I0416824

S. HRG. 112–871

THE STATE OF CHRONIC DISEASE PREVENTION

HEARING

OF THE

COMMITTEE ON HEALTH, EDUCATION, LABOR, AND PENSIONS

UNITED STATES SENATE

ONE HUNDRED TWELFTH CONGRESS

FIRST SESSION

ON

EXAMINING THE STATE OF CHRONIC DISEASE PREVENTION

OCTOBER 12, 2011

Printed for the use of the Committee on Health, Education, Labor, and Pensions

Available via the World Wide Web: http://www.gpo.gov/fdsys/

U.S. GOVERNMENT PRINTING OFFICE

87–561 PDF   WASHINGTON : 2014

For sale by the Superintendent of Documents, U.S. Government Printing Office
Internet: bookstore.gpo.gov   Phone: toll free (866) 512–1800; DC area (202) 512–1800
Fax: (202) 512–2250   Mail: Stop SSOP, Washington, DC 20402–0001

(II)

CONTENTS

STATEMENTS

WEDNESDAY, OCTOBER 12, 2011

Page

THE STATE OF CHRONIC DISEASE PREVENTION

WEDNESDAY, OCTOBER 12, 2011

U.S. SENATE,
COMMITTEE ON HEALTH, EDUCATION, LABOR, AND PENSIONS,
Washington, DC.

The committee met, pursuant to notice, at 2:31 p.m., in room SD–430, Dirksen Senate Office Building, Hon. Tom Harkin, chairman of the committee, presiding.

Present: Senators Harkin, Mikulski, Franken, Whitehouse, Blumenthal, and Roberts.

OPENING STATEMENT OF SENATOR HARKIN

The CHAIRMAN. The Senate Committee on Health, Education, Labor, and Pensions will come to order.

Chronic disease presents one of the greatest challenges to the public health of the American people. Research shows that almost one out of every two adults has at least one chronic disease. We also know that nearly one-fourth of individuals with chronic disease have one or more daily activity limitations. It's a staggering fact that 7 out of 10 deaths among Americans are related to chronic illnesses.

Our Nation's fiscal well-being is also impacted by chronic disease. Of the more than $2 trillion we spend on healthcare, 75 percent is accounted for by individuals with chronic conditions. In the workplace, these conditions account for nearly $1 trillion in lost productivity each year. Chronic disease is a huge cost to both private and public sectors and a major contributor to our deficits and our debt.

A major gap exists between what we know about chronic disease prevention and what we're actually doing about it. There are many examples of effective, evidence-based prevention programs that we will hear about from our witnesses. We need to apply these proven approaches to prevent chronic diseases from developing in the first place, which will improve health and restrain healthcare costs.

An important tool to address chronic disease is the implementation of proven prevention programs in local communities. Targeted, evidence-based community prevention activities can have an enormous impact on chronic disease, while at the same time being cost-effective. A study by the Trust for America's Health titled Prevention for a Healthier America found that investing $10 per person in proven community-based programs to increase physical activity, improve nutrition, and prevent tobacco use could save the Nation about $16 billion annually within 5 years.

The Community Transformation Grant program and the Affordable Care Act helps communities to implement evidence-based strategies that prevent the development of chronic diseases. Through this program, communities develop public-private partnerships and collaborate to tailor health promotion initiatives that meet the unique needs of their residents in addressing chronic disease. This helps turn the environment in which local residents live, work, play, and raise their families into one that provides a greater array of healthy choices, making the healthy choice the easy choice.

I've often said, it's easier to be unhealthy and harder to be healthy, and shouldn't we turn that dynamic around? Shouldn't it be easier to be healthy and harder to be unhealthy? That's why the Prevention and Public Health Fund, which I authored in the Affordable Care Act, is so fundamental to addressing the gap that exists between what is and what can be done to address chronic illness.

The Prevention Fund supports evidence-based health promotion programs. However, this fund is only a small down payment in comparison to the size of the problem. Some critics have called the fund a "slush fund." Well, that's nonsense. Let me give just a few examples of investments made possible by this fund to address chronic disease.

In Alabama, funding is being used to make Mobile County smoke-free, and tobacco quit lines and media are helping residents to live tobacco-free. Thanks to the fund, South Carolina has started a statewide Farm-to-School program that brings fresh fruits and vegetables to children in over 1,000 schools in South Carolina.

Another tool in addressing chronic disease is the use of evidence-based clinical preventative services. We significantly increased the availability of these critical activities in the Affordable Care Act by requiring first dollar coverage of recommended preventative services. Many Americans are already benefiting from these important evidence-based preventative services and wellness visits, which will help lower costs, prevent disease, and save lives. Now, these services also make great economic sense. For example, for every $1 we spend on the full course of childhood vaccines we save $16.50 in future healthcare costs.

Businesses have not traditionally been players in the field of wellness and disease prevention. But this is rapidly changing. I find this very, very encouraging, because corporate America has the expertise, the resources, and the enlightened self-interest to make a huge difference in the way we approach healthcare in this country. That's why I included a provision in the ACA that makes it easier for businesses to push more of their healthcare investments upstream, helping employees to stay healthy and stay out of the hospital.

Proven prevention efforts need to occur not only in the doctor's office, but where people live and work and go to school. American families also recognize the importance of these services in preventing chronic disease. According to a national survey conducted by Lake Research Partners, prevention and wellness resonate with Americans on a core value level and enjoy very broad support. People know that prevention saves both lives and money.

I'm looking forward to the testimony of our expert witnesses who approach this important issue from a variety of perspectives, all with the goal of transforming our current sick care system into a genuine healthcare system, one that emphasizes wellness and prevention and public health. And so I thank everyone for being here, and I am looking forward to the testimony.

Now I'll yield to Senator Roberts for an opening statement.

STATEMENT OF SENATOR ROBERTS

Senator ROBERTS. Mr. Chairman, thank you so much for holding this hearing today. I apologize for being late. That's a chronic disease that I've had for some years. And thank you for your leadership on this.

And I want to thank also all of our witnesses for appearing before our committee and your continued commitment to prevention and to public health. I think we all know the statistics related to chronic disease. I know the chairman has spoken of that. Billions and billions of dollars are spent each year to treat these conditions and the efforts to prevent their occurrence. I think that we all have a story of someone, ourselves or a loved one, affected by a chronic disease.

If only wishing made it so, we would have prevented and cured many of these conditions many years ago. Unfortunately, we still struggle to prevent and treat chronic conditions. But science has evolved our understanding of how chronic conditions can be mitigated or avoided, which leads us to today's discussion on the state of chronic disease prevention and the implementation of the Prevention and Public Health Fund authorized under the new healthcare law.

I do share some of my colleagues' questions about the implementation of many parts of the law, including the fund, and the current discussions on deficit reduction and spending reductions continue to evaluate where this fund should fall into the prioritization of Federal funding. But I am hopeful that today's hearing and the testimony of today's witnesses will help us better inform that assessment.

The reality of our current combination of public health priorities and economic challenges leave us with no option. As the saying used to be, just throw spaghetti at the wall and see what sticks. That is to say any funding, especially Public Health and Prevention Funding, must be very carefully distributed and the outcomes clearly identified in order to prioritize the few resources that are available. That's unfortunate, but that's the way things are today.

Additionally, if we determine that the funding is a priority, it is essential to ensure oversight of these dollars to make sure that metrics are in place for measuring the outcomes associated with public health and prevention programs and that they are meeting and exceeding the minimum metrics. In my opinion, this is the only way to ensure that we are reducing costs yet saving lives and prioritizing Federal dollars appropriately.

I look forward to hearing from our witnesses today and again thank the chairman for his leadership in holding the hearing.

The CHAIRMAN. Thank you very much, Senator Roberts, and I agree with everything you said. I think it's got to be evidence-based and make sure that we're getting a good return on the dollar that we've invested.

Senator ROBERTS. Yes, sir.

The CHAIRMAN. We have two panels today, two great panels. Our first panel will be just one witness, our Assistant Secretary, and then we'll have the second panel.

Our first panel will be Dr. Howard Koh, Assistant Secretary for Health at the Department of Health and Human Services. Dr. Koh is a well-recognized expert in the field of public health.

Before being confirmed as the 14th Assistant Secretary, he served as Professor at the Harvard School of Public Health, Director of the Harvard School of Public Health Center for Public Health Preparedness, and as Commissioner of Public Health for the Commonwealth of Massachusetts. As Assistant Secretary, Dr. Koh is dedicated to the mission of creating better public health systems for prevention and care in the United States.

Dr. Koh, we all know your wonderful background. Your statement will be made a part of the record in its entirety. And if you could sum it up in 5 to 10 minutes, we'd be appreciative so we can get to questions and answers.

STATEMENT OF HOWARD K. KOH, M.D., M.P.H., ASSISTANT SECRETARY FOR HEALTH, U.S. DEPARTMENT OF HEALTH AND HUMAN SERVICES, WASHINGTON, DC

Dr. KOH. Thank you so much, Chairman Harkin, Ranking Member Roberts, and distinguished members of the committee. I'm Dr. Howard Koh, the Assistant Secretary for Health. I want to start by thanking you for holding this critical hearing on prevention.

Promoting disease prevention is absolutely crucial to reducing suffering and death in our country, improving the health of our Nation, and addressing the enormous costs of healthcare. The passage of the Affordable Care Act and with it the creation of the Prevention and Public Health Fund represents a pivotal action by Congress and the Federal Government that will promote prevention and improve the overall health and well-being of all Americans for the future.

I'd like to start by thanking you, Senator Harkin, for your vital leadership on this important issue. You have been leading the charge to promote prevention and wellness for your entire career, and we are all deeply in your debt. And I also want to thank all the committee members, because this is such a crucial issue for our Nation's public health.

Today, our country is facing an epidemic of unprecedented magnitude, that is, the overwhelming burden of chronic diseases throughout our country. As you heard from the chairman, 7 out of 10 deaths in the United States are due to chronic conditions. Heart disease, cancer, and stroke account for more than 50 percent of all deaths each year. Nearly half of all adults in our Nation have at least one chronic illness. And we need greater attention and commitment to prevention more than ever before.

For example, rates of obesity in our country are increasing with more than one in three adults in this category, as well as almost one in every five children. As you can see from the chart on the right, with the highest obesity rates in red, the epidemic of obesity is engulfing our Nation over time.

Astoundingly, chronic disease is responsible for more than 75 percent of the more than $2.5 trillion we spend annually on healthcare. Confronting the massive impact of chronic disease on both our Nation's health and our economy is imperative to saving lives and bringing down healthcare costs.

My own commitment to prevention began decades ago as I was starting my career as a physician and clinician. As a young physician, it was absolutely heart wrenching, starting then and over the next three decades, to care for so many patients who were suffering and dying preventable deaths. It was clear to me, and I know to all of us, that as a country, we need a better national approach to finding disease earlier or preventing it in the first place. These are themes I've been very committed to in my career as a researcher, physician, State health commissioner, and now as the Assistant Secretary for Health.

We know that preventing disease can save lives and reduce suffering. And by focusing on the most prevalent chronic diseases, such as heart disease, cancer, stroke, and diabetes, and addressing behaviors that fuel these conditions, such as tobacco use, poor diet, physical inactivity, and alcohol abuse, we can make a profound impact on reducing the harm caused by chronic diseases.

The economic argument for investing in prevention is also compelling. Using evidence-based interventions can improve health and prevent unnecessary suffering and also potentially save money. One recent study in the journal, Lancet, just published, estimates that an average 1 percent reduction in body mass index, BMI, across the United States could potentially avoid up to 2.4 million cases of diabetes, 1.7 million cases of cardiovascular disease, and up to 127,000 cases of cancer.

However, only an estimated 3 percent or less of all healthcare dollars in the United States right now are dedicated to these scientifically proven prevention strategies. This is barely the proverbial ounce of prevention that we all have talked about in the past. By investing in prevention, as the Senator said, we can transition our current medical care system from one of sick care to one that's based on prevention and wellness.

We are grateful that the Affordable Care Act represents a transformative opportunity to bring prevention to the forefront of the Nation's priorities. And one of the most important commitments in that Act is the creation of the Prevention and Public Health Fund. The fund represents our most significant investment to step up and scale up effective prevention and public health measures in our Nation's history. And despite only being in existence for 2 years, it's already making positive impact in a broad range of areas.

The fund allows us to make targeted, high-priority investments in areas of obesity, tobacco, HIV, immunization, hospital-required conditions, substance abuse, behavioral health, as well as build a stronger primary care workforce, surveillance systems, and laboratories. And these investments, along with Federal expertise and partnerships with State and local leaders, can best address the needs of our communities across the country.

As you know, the fund started in fiscal year 2010 with $500 million, a figure that rose, as required by statute, to $750 million in fiscal year 2011. And these funds are being used in the statue, as noted in the language,

> "to provide for expanded and sustained national investments in prevention and public health programs, to improve health, and help restrain the rate of growth in the private and public sector healthcare costs."

The fund has made strides in leaving a legacy to help make the healthier choice the easier choice in communities. And just as an example, recently, the CDC just announced over $100 million to be used for Community Transformation Grants. These programs will help State and local communities address root causes of poor health, improve prevention at both the clinical and community levels so that Americans can lead healthier and more productive lives.

The Affordable Care Act also mobilizes national partners in prevention, such as a new National Prevention, Public Health, and Health Promotion Council, a new National Prevention Strategy, and brings together partners in 17 Federal agencies to prioritize these efforts in public health in what we call a Health In All Policies approach.

In closing, the burden and urgent threat of chronic disease constitutes one of the major public health challenges of the 21st Century. We can prevent future death and suffering through strong scientific approaches that incorporate evidence-based and affordable population-wide interventions.

The Affordable Care Act and especially the Prevention and Public Health Fund are helping us reach our goal of transitioning our Nation away from being a sick care system to one that prizes prevention and public health in the community. We are committed to furthering this important work and look forward to sharing more success stories with you in the future.

Thank you very much, and I'd be very pleased to take some questions.

[The prepared statement of Dr. Koh follows:]

PREPARED STATEMENT OF HOWARD K. KOH, M.D., M.P.H

Good afternoon, Chairman Harkin and Ranking Member Enzi. I am Dr. Howard K. Koh, the Assistant Secretary for Health at the U.S. Department of Health and Human Services. I would like to thank you for holding this important hearing on the critical role of prevention in improving the health of Americans and how the Prevention and Public Health Fund that was created by the Affordable Care Act supports our efforts to prioritize prevention across our programs and policies. The passage of the Affordable Care Act and with it the creation of the Prevention and Public Health Fund represents one of the most important actions by Congress and the Federal Government to promote prevention to improve the overall health and well-being of the American people. It manifests an unprecedented commitment to ensuring that all Americans are able to achieve their potential by realizing the highest standard of health. Also, I would like to take this opportunity to thank you, Senator Harkin, for your leadership on this important issue. You have been leading the charge to promote prevention and wellness for your entire career, and we are all indebted to you for your tremendous work on this important topic.

As the Assistant Secretary for Health, I am tasked with advancing prevention nationwide. Promoting prevention and its crucial role in improving the health of individuals, and communities, has truly been a life-long passion of mine. Before assuming my current position, I spent more than 30 years as a physician, caring for patients. When I began my career as a clinician, I set out to alleviate the pain and suffering of my patients to the best of my ability. However, as I provided care for more and more people facing serious medical problems, I came to realize that a significant number of the problems my patients faced were preventable. Thus, I became intensely interested in finding ways to educate my patients about prevention so that they, and their loved ones, could maintain healthy lifestyles and avoid unnecessary pain, sickness and early death.

During my tenure as the Commissioner of Public Health for the Commonwealth of Massachusetts, one of my key priorities was to promote prevention efforts throughout the State. I worked with the health care sector, the business sector, other government sectors, community-based organizations and private citizens to raise awareness about community prevention and preventive health care services. To support these efforts, we worked closely with the Federal Government, including the CDC, on many of these initiatives. The Federal Government has been a partner for many years in promoting prevention, and I am committed to accelerating these efforts as the Assistant Secretary for Health.

CHRONIC DISEASE AND THE UNITED STATES

Today, the United States is facing an epidemic of unprecedented magnitude: the sky-rocketing prevalence of chronic disease throughout our Nation. Seven out of every ten deaths in the United States are due to some form of chronic condition. Heart disease, cancer and stroke account for more than 50 percent of all deaths each year. Nearly half of all adults in our Nation have at least one chronic illness. Rates of obesity are increasing, with more than one in three adults fitting the clinical definition of obese, and almost one in every five children being categorized as obese. Diabetes rates are also on the rise. If current trends continue, one out of every three babies born today will suffer from diabetes at some point in their life. Indeed, chronic disease impacts all Americans, but not equally. Rates of chronic disease among racial and ethnic minorities, and among lower-income Americans, are higher than the national average and thus are of particular concern. Racial and ethnic minority communities experience higher rates of heart disease, stroke, cancer, obesity and diabetes. Within the African-American and Hispanic demographic, nearly 40 percent of children are overweight or obese.

Chronic disease impacts not only the health of the individual and their families, but it has a broader impact on our communities and the economy. Astoundingly, chronic disease is responsible for more than 75 percent of the more than $2.5 trillion we spend annually on health care.[1] Specifically, nationwide health care costs for all cardiovascular diseases are $442 billion annually[2]; diabetes-associated costs are approximately $174 billion annually[3]; obesity-related costs are approximately $147 billion annually[4]; and lung disease costs are approximately $154 billion annually.[5] In fact, cigarette smoking costs the Nation an astounding $193 billion in health costs and lost productivity each year.[6] Society—and business—also incurs the indirect costs of these conditions, including absenteeism, disability and reduced productivity.

With employer-based health insurance covering almost 160 million workers under age 65, preventing disease and improving health outcomes is a financial imperative for many businesses. The Almanac of Chronic Disease by the Partnership to Fight Chronic Disease documented that chronic disease causes the loss of $1 trillion[7] in economic output annually. Furthermore, individuals serving as caregivers to loved ones suffering from chronic disease also represent an undercounted economic cost of chronic disease that runs into the tens of billions of dollars annually. The Almanac of Chronic Disease, for example, estimates that lost productivity associated with caregiving activities totals approximately $91 billion annually. Confronting the massive impact of chronic disease on our Nation's health, and our economy, is imperative to bringing down health care costs and improving the lives of our citizens.

---

[1] *http://www.cdc.gov/chronicdisease/resources/publications/AAG/chronic.htm.*

[2] AHA Policy Statement: Forecasting the Future of Cardiovascular Disease in the U.S. (January 2011: *http://circ.ahajournals.org/content/123/8/933.full.pdf+html.*

[3] American Diabetes Association. Direct and Indirect Costs of Diabetes in the United States. American Diabetes Association Web site. Available at *http://www.diabetes.org/diabetes-basics/diabetes-statistics/.*

[4] Finkelstein, E.A., Trogdon, J.G., Cohen, J.W., and Dietz, W. Annual medical spending attributable to obesity: payer and service-specific estimates. Health Affairs 2009; 28:w822–w831.

[5] National Heart, Lung, and Blood Institute. Morbidity and Mortality: 2004 Chart Book on Cardiovascular, Lung, and Blood Diseases. Bethesda, MD: National Institutes of Health, 2004.

[6] *http://www.cdc.gov/tobacco/data_statistics/fact_sheets/fast_facts/.*

[7] *http://www.fightchronicdisease.org/sites/default/files/docs/2009AlmanacofChronicDisease_updated81009.pdf.*

PREVENTING DISEASE: VALUE FOR HEALTH AND THE ECONOMY

Preventing disease can save lives and money. With health care costs on the perpetual rise, investments that reduce costs and improve health outcomes are critically important. By focusing on the most prevalent chronic diseases (heart disease, cancer, stroke and diabetes) and addressing behaviors that contribute to these conditions (tobacco use, poor diet, physical inactivity and alcohol abuse), we can make a profound impact on reducing the harm caused by chronic disease.

Here are just a few examples:

• Health care costs for smokers, people who are obese, and those who have diabetes are $2,000, $1,400, and $6,600 per year higher for each person with these conditions, respectively. Health care costs saved from preventing these diseases reduce health insurance premiums.

• A proven program that prevents diabetes can save costs within 3 years.[8]

• A 5 percent reduction in the prevalence of hypertension would save $25 billion in 5 years.[9]

The economic argument for investing in prevention is compelling. The use of evidence-based interventions can improve health and prevent unnecessary suffering, while at the same time, save money for both the government and the private sector. According to the CDC, for example, there is a $10 return on investment for every dollar spent on childhood vaccinations. Vaccination of children and adolescents prevent approximately 20 million cases of disease each year and save as many as 42,000 lives on an annual basis. Immunizing children born in the United States each year costs about $7 billion and saves $21 billion in direct costs and $55 billion in indirect costs [10] In another example, the implementation of CDC's guidelines for preventing blood stream infections could potentially save $414 million annually in excess health care costs and $1.8 billion annually estimated cumulative excess health care costs prevents 25,000 infections from occurring; and saves approximately 4,500 lives.[11]

Despite the indisputable wisdom of investing in prevention, currently less than 1 percent of all health care dollars spent in the United States are dedicated to these scientifically proven, effective strategies. If we managed heart disease better, for example, by 2023 we could reduce associated health care costs by $76 billion. And, if stronger prevention and care management systems are implemented across the Nation for the seven leading chronic diseases, our economy could see $1 trillion in savings by 2023.[12] By investing in prevention, we can transition our current medical care system from a sick care system to one based on prevention and wellness.

PREVENTION AND THE AFFORDABLE CARE ACT

The passage of the Affordable Care Act was an historic moment that represented a major commitment to ensure all Americans have access to high quality and affordable health care while focusing on promoting the health and well-being of communities. The Affordable Care Act is a landmark law that grants individuals more control over their health care, and brings down the cost of health care for both families and businesses. At the same time, the Affordable Care Act also represents a once in a generation opportunity to bring prevention to the forefront of the dialogue about health care and the cost of care. Under the Affordable Care Act, people in traditional Medicare as well as individuals joining private insurance plans will receive recommended preventive services with no cost-sharing requirements for patients. The Affordable Care Act also provides States the option to provide these services in Medicaid, with incentives for eliminating cost-sharing. The law also requires new health plans to cover important services for infants and children as outlined in the Bright Futures Guidelines and preventive services for women across their life-span, included as part of HRSA supported Guidelines for Women's Preventive

---

[8] Rigorous economic models have demonstrated that structured lifestyle interventions to prevent diabetes can be cost-saving within 2 to 3 years time if the direct costs of the intervention can be reduced to $250–$300/participant/year. Ackermann, R.T., Marrero, D.G., Hicks, K.A., Hoerger, T.J., Sorensen, S., Zhang, P., Engelgau, M.M., Ratner, R.E., and Herman, W H. (2006). An evaluation of cost sharing to finance a diet and physical activity intervention to prevent diabetes. Diabetes care, 29(6):1237–41. And Ackermann, R.T., Finch, E.A., Brizendine, E., Zhou, H., and Marrero, D.G. (2008). Translating the diabetes prevention program into the community. The DEPLOY pilot study. Am J Prev Med, 35(4):357–63.

[9] Ormond, B.A., Spillman, B.C., Waidmann, T.A., Caswell, K.J., and Tereschchenko, B. Potential National and State Medical Care Savings from Primary Disease Prevention. Am J Public Health 2011, 101(1): 157–64.

[10] Preliminary results, updated from Zhou, F., Arch of Pediatric and Adolescent Medicine.

[11] http://www.cdc.gov/mmwr/pdf/wk/mm60e0301.pdf.

[12] http://www.fightchronicdisease.org/resources/almanac-chronic-disease-0.

Services, without co-pays, co-insurance rates, or deductibles. So far in 2011, nearly 20.5 million people with Medicare reviewed their health status at a free Annual Wellness Visit or received other preventive services with no deductible or cost sharing this year, and as many as 41 million Americans in new health plans are also benefiting from free preventive services because of the law.

The Affordable Care Act, however, recognizes health goes beyond the clinical setting. As such, the Affordable Care Act creates the National Prevention, Health Promotion, and Public Health Council (National Prevention Council) to provide coordination and leadership at the Federal level and among all executive agencies regarding prevention, wellness, and health promotion practices. It is composed of the heads of 17 Federal agencies and chaired by Surgeon General Regina Benjamin. The National Prevention Council released the National Prevention and Health Promotion Strategy as a comprehensive plan for Federal, State, local and private partners to work together to help increase the number of Americans who are healthy at every stage of life. The Strategy recognizes good health comes not just from receiving quality medical care but from stopping disease before it starts. Good health also comes from clean air and water, safe outdoor spaces for physical activity, safe worksites, healthy foods, violence-free environments and healthy homes. Prevention should be woven into all aspects of our lives, including where and how we live, learn, work and play. Everyone—businesses, educators, health care institutions, government, communities and every single American—has a role in creating a healthier nation. Investments in prevention across the life span complement and support treatment and care. Prevention policies and programs can be cost-effective, reduce health care costs, and improve productivity.

The Strategy provides four broad strategic directions to improve prevention and wellness in order to have a healthier America, including building healthy and safe community environments; expanding quality preventive services in both clinical and community settings; empowering people to make healthy choices; and eliminating health disparities.

One of the most important commitments in the Affordable Care Act to help HHS achieve such goals is the investment in public health and community prevention programs made possible by the creation of the Prevention and Public Health Fund (the Prevention Fund, or Fund). The Fund represents our most significant investment to promote and scale up effective public health and prevention measures in our Nation's history. Despite only being in existence for 2 years, the Fund is already making a positive impact on public health, prevention and wellness across the Nation.

The Fund allows us to make targeted, high priority investments across a spectrum of prevention and public health initiatives. Primary prevention programs work at the community level, and they employ local scientists, epidemiologists, laboratorians, and others to control diseases before people end up in a hospital or acute care centers. Fund investments represent a unique blend of Federal expertise, technical assistance and data with State and local, on-the-ground experts who best understand the needs of their respective communities. With the Fund, we are supporting, expanding and accelerating our commitment to innovative and effective prevention programs that impact people's lives on a daily basis.

The Fund currently supports public health programs to prevent and reduce obesity, tobacco use, heart disease, diabetes and cancer, strengthen the public health workforce, modernize and improve vaccine systems, and track outbreaks of disease across the country. Our partners in health organizations across the Nation are having a real impact that will be felt in both lives saved and costs avoided.

The Fund provided $500 million in fiscal year funding for critical initiatives focused on the training of new primary care providers to help meet the needs of a growing and aging population, and provide essential primary and preventive care. Funding also is enabling us to embrace smarter more strategic approaches within current programs. As just one example, to further the goals of the *National HIV/ AIDS Strategy for the United States* which calls for improved coordination across all levels of government, CDC used resources from the fund to launch a pilot initiative in the 12 communities with the highest AIDS prevalence to test and evaluate new approaches to integrating planning for prevention and care services. In addition to the investment in building our primary care workforce, our fiscal year 2010 investments laid the groundwork for achieving three primary objectives:

• Empower communities to reduce heart attacks, cancer, stroke, injuries and more—the leading causes of disability and death.

• Enhance State and local capacity to detect and respond to disease threats and manage scarce resources.

• Produce information for action—what prevention programs work and performance of the health system—so we can increase the health value of our health investments.

These objectives were the focus of our fiscal year investments, when the size of the fund increased to $750 million, enabling HHS to work with States, tribes and local governments to continue many of the strategic investments made in the previous year, and at the same time expand investments to support prevention and public health initiatives at every level of government. In fiscal year 2011, the Fund continued support for community and clinical prevention efforts, public health infrastructure development, and research and tracking initiatives to evaluate the efficacy of efforts related to the program. Initiatives receiving funding include:

• **Community and State Prevention ($222 million).** Implement the Community Transformation Grant (CTG) program and strengthen other programs to support State and community initiatives to use evidence-based interventions to prevent heart attacks, strokes, cancer and other conditions by reducing tobacco use, preventing obesity, and reducing health disparities. Launch a consolidated chronic disease prevention grant program.

• **Tobacco Prevention ($60 million).** Implement anti-tobacco media campaigns that have been proven to reduce tobacco use, telephone-based tobacco cessation services, and outreach programs targeted toward vulnerable populations, consistent with HHS' Tobacco Control Strategic Action Plan.

• **Obesity Prevention and Fitness ($16 million).** Advance activities to improve nutrition and increase physical activity to promote healthy lifestyles and reduce obesity-related conditions and costs. These activities will implement recommendations of the President's Childhood Obesity Task Force.

• **Access to Critical Wellness and Preventive Health Services ($112 million).** Increase awareness of new prevention benefits made available by the Affordable Care Act. Expand immunization and strengthen employer participation in wellness programs.

• **Reduce the Impact of Substance Abuse and Mental Illness ($70 million).** Assist communities with the coordination and integration of primary care services into publicly funded community mental health and other community-based behavioral health settings.

• **Public Health Infrastructure and Capacity ($92 million).** Support State, local, and tribal public health infrastructure to advance health promotion and disease prevention and improve detection and response to disease outbreaks by improving epidemiology and laboratory capacity, information technology, public health workforce training, and policy development.

• **Public Health Workforce ($45 million).** Support training of public health providers to advance preventive medicine, health promotion and disease prevention and epidemiology in medically underserved communities.

• **Health Care Surveillance and Research ($133 million).** Improve the evidence base for prevention and public health by improving data collection and analysis (including on environmental health hazards), and investing in rigorous review of evidence on the effectiveness of both clinical prevention services and community interventions.

Already, the Fund has made strides in prevention and public health in a way that will leave a legacy of commitment and success for the future. This year, we invested over $100 million of the Fund in Community Transformation Grants (CTGs). This program provides direct support to State and local communities to help tackle the root causes of poor health so Americans can lead healthier, more productive lives. The grantees will work to implement proven prevention activities and build capacity in their community to support sustainable initiatives in the future. Grantees will work to address the following priority areas: tobacco-free living; active living and healthy eating; and quality clinical and other preventive services, specifically prevention and control of high blood pressure and high cholesterol. Grantees, who are expected to have a direct impact on up to 120 million Americans, will use these funds to improve where Americans live, work, play, and go to school, and to reduce chronic diseases, such as heart disease, stroke and diabetes, which account for a significant portion of the health care costs in the United States.

By promoting healthy lifestyles, especially among population groups experiencing the highest rates of chronic disease, these grants will help improve health, reduce health disparities, and control health care spending. Within the CTG program, there is a clear focus on addressing health care disparities. More than half of the recipients intend to target African-American and Latino populations, and over one in three of the grantees will focus specifically on American Indians/Alaska Natives. Almost all grantees will include initiatives focused on children, and nearly 20 percent of the programs will include efforts to improve the health of older adults. And consistent with the program's authorization, at least 20 percent of grant funds are directed to rural and frontier areas to help them address their unique health issues. The CTG program is a direct investment of Prevention and Public Health Fund dollars into our communities that will improve the health of our society. CTGs will allow cities and States to innovate and implement specifically tailored interventions in their own communities in order to promote health, increase prevention and reduce the burden of chronic disease throughout our Nation.

With funding recently awarded, communities across America are initiating work to tackle critical health problems. Selected examples include:

• In Minnesota, the Hennepin County Human Services and Public Health Department is implementing comprehensive tobacco-free policies in public housing, and increasing daily physical activity in school-settings by implementing a Safe Routes to School program and adopting Active Recess systems at elementary and middle schools.

• The Iowa Department of Public Health is improving school-based nutrition and the quality and amount of physical activity in schools. Iowa is also increasing health provider awareness of high blood pressure and high cholesterol through new clinical tools and systems.

• The North Carolina Division of Public Health will work toward increasing the number of convenience stores that offer fresh produce, and increase the number of communities that support farmers' markets, mobile markets, and farm stands. North Carolina will also increase the number of healthcare organizations that support tobacco use screening, referral and cessation.

• The Sault Saint Marie Tribe of Chippewa Indians will create a region-wide Food Policy Council to increase accessibility, availability, affordability and identification of healthful foods in communities; improve the quality and amount of physical education and physical activity in schools; and support workplace policies and programs that increase physical activity and work to increase bicycling and walking for transportation and pleasure.

• The West Virginia Bureau for Public Health is working with the States' clinical sector to assure improvement in control of high blood pressure and high LDL-cholesterol.

In addition to partnering with State and local governments, and others working in communities across the United States, the Department is committed to partnering with the private sector to promote prevention and reduce the prevalence of chronic disease. At the end of last month, the Department announced a workplace wellness initiative to improve the health of workers and their families. The CDC recently awarded a contract that will help an estimated 70 to 100 small, mid-size, and large employers create and expand workplace programs aimed at achieving three goals: reduce the risk of chronic disease among employees and their families through evidence-based workplace health interventions and promising practices; promote sustainable and replicable workplace health activities; and promote peer-to-peer healthy business mentoring. These efforts—focused on changing programs, policies, benefits, environmental supports and links to outside community prevention efforts—will help CDC learn about best practices and replicable models that can be disseminated to the business community to inform their efforts to adopt cost-saving preventive measures.

The President included recommendations to the Joint Select Committee on Deficit Reduction that would prioritize investments within the Prevention and Public Health Fund. At the same time, the Federal Government will continue to invest strategically in areas of national importance, such as prevention. To this end, President Obama's recently released deficit reduction plan would allow for significant investments in prevention and public health activities of more than $6 billion over 5 years and $13.8 billion over 10 years, while providing $3.5 billion in savings. Even with this reduction in the Fund's size, the Federal Government will still be able to make significant investments in prevention and tackle the urgent threat and challenge chronic disease presents to our society. We, at the Department, look forward to continuing to execute this important plan.

In addition to the Prevention and Public Health Fund, the Obama administration has made a significant commitment to combating childhood obesity so that children born today can grow up healthier and able to pursue their dreams. The First Lady has already been successful in bringing nutrition and healthy lifestyle messages to the forefront of the national conversation through *Let's Move!*, a comprehensive initiative dedicated to solving the challenge of childhood obesity within a generation.

Building on the strong foundation of the Affordable Care Act, the Department of Health and Human Services launched the "Million Hearts™" initiative with other

Federal, State and local government agencies, and a broad range of private-sector partners. The goal of this program is to prevent 1 million heart attacks and strokes over the next 5 years by implementing proven, effective, inexpensive interventions. The Department is committed to developing and implementing robust and multi-faceted approaches to prevention. By coordinating the multiple initiatives focused on prevention and wellness across the government, and joining with partners at the State and local level, we can bring about fundamental change that ensures a brighter and healthier future for all Americans.

CONCLUSION

In closing, the burden and urgent threat of chronic disease constitutes one of the major public health challenges of the 21st century. The incidence and impacts of preventable diseases can be largely reduced with an approach that incorporates evidence-based, affordable population-wide interventions. The Affordable Care Act and, especially, the Prevention and Public Health Fund, is helping us make significant progress in our efforts to transition our Nation's health care system away from being a sick care system. In the last 2 years, the Department has used the Prevention and Public Health Fund to make important strategic investments in promoting preventive health care and community health, and to improving our Nation's public health infrastructure. We are committed to continuing this important work and look forward to sharing more success stories with you in the future. Thank you. I am now happy to take questions.

The CHAIRMAN. Thank you very much, Mr. Secretary. We'll start rounds of 5-minute questions.

Mr. Secretary, you've outlined in your testimony, which I read last night, all the different things you're doing with these funds. You say the fund allows us to make targeted, high-priority investments across a spectrum of prevention and public health initiatives. You list all of those.

Would you address what's been published and what some people have said—they've just called this a slush fund. I'm not certain what that definition is, but it doesn't sound good. So how would you respond to someone saying it's just a slush fund? What's your response to that?

Dr. KOH. First, Mr. Chairman, we have so many urgent threats with respect to preventable conditions that we have all already discussed in the opening minutes of this very important hearing. We know that prevention works. We have science and evidence that interventions can make a difference and save lives and reduce suffering and begin to reverse these rising healthcare costs.

But the challenge has been that we haven't had the opportunity or the resources to make those interventions available to community and local leaders so they can make a difference around the country. So we are administering these efforts according to strict guidelines. We are following the directives of the statute passed by Congress and put into law.

We have strict adherence to accountability and to proper uses of these funds so that we can support State and local efforts. And we view this as a partnership where we help local and State leaders move prevention and advance these evidence-based interventions, and that's the whole theme of this effort.

The CHAIRMAN. I listened very closely to what my friend from Kansas had to say, and I agreed with him that we want to see evidence-based processes going forward. We want the collection of data. Are you comfortable with that, the way we're proceeding, that we will have good evidence-based processes?

Dr. KOH: We have not only implementation of evidence-based interventions, but also very strong and rigorous evaluation strategies embedded with each grant. And we are committed to seeing outcomes and strong evidence of what works and what works even better with respect to prevention. So this is a great investment in prevention, in public health, and in the rigor of science. And that's what we're advancing with these efforts.

The CHAIRMAN. Mr. Secretary, a number of times—and using my own phraseology—runs have been made on this fund to take money out of it to use it for something else. You mentioned just one initiative that you started. You call it the Million Hearts Initiative with other Federal, State, and local governments. The goal was to prevent a million heart attacks and strokes for the next 5 years by implementing proven, effective, inexpensive interventions.

Could you just talk a little bit about that? If this fund is cut down, what happens to that kind of an initiative?

Dr. KOH. We all understand that cardiovascular disease is the leading killer in this country. We know that so much of this is absolutely preventable. We know that a lot of heart disease and stroke is driven by issues such as blood pressure control, cholesterol control, and particularly tobacco dependence.

If we set national goals, as has been done in this so-called Million Hearts Initiative just unveiled several weeks ago by the Secretary, and really galvanize national attention on reducing those risk factors, we can see an even further decline in cardiovascular disease deaths in the future than we've had before. And we view this as a critical way of reducing suffering and also reducing health disparities in the country. There are major disparities with respect to cardiovascular disease that we need to address as well.

The CHAIRMAN. Mr. Secretary, I'll bring this up at the next panel because we have experts from different disease groups. But on diabetes, could you address yourself to the looming prospect of how many people are going to be getting diabetes, young people? You mentioned it. Today, you said, one out of every three babies will suffer from diabetes—even higher among African-Americans and Hispanics, almost one out of every two.

How would this fund approach that? How are we going to prevent that from happening?

Dr. KOH. The rising obesity rates are a tremendous societal challenge right now. And the rising obesity rates fuel Type 2 diabetes, heart disease, stroke, even some forms of cancer. And so we know that tackling the obesity challenge for children and adults is a way of preventing diabetes and cancer and heart disease as well.

For example, in these Community Transformation Grants that have just been announced by the CDC, there are directives for grantees to work on reducing obesity rates in their respective communities through a Health In All Policies approach, and that's prevention at its very best. And we expect to see big payoffs in the future and reverse this trend, because otherwise, the health of our country is greatly at risk.

The CHAIRMAN. Thank you, Mr. Secretary. My time is up.

Senator Roberts.

Senator ROBERTS. Thank you, Mr. Chairman, and Doctor, several times over.

In discussing the special initiative on the funding from the fund—and the chairman is exactly correct. Folks have been using

14

this fund as a bank, and that's not for what it was intended. But you used statements that are very familiar to the committee and to everybody here in the hearing room and the Public Health Committee, like increased awareness, support State and local public health infrastructure, advanced activities.

I know that when we get to the challenges of the Super Committee on what this committee and other committees are going to have to recommend to the Super Committee, or vice versa, they're going to ask with limited dollars, "Can you specify what each of these dollars were used for and detail the pragmatic use of these funds?" What would you advise us to say in that regard?

Dr. KOH. Thank you for that question, Senator. When we look at the challenge of public health in our country and see how much suffering is due to illness that could be and should be prevented, one has to reach the conclusion that we need more of an emphasis on prevention as well as treatment. And we view that new emphasis as one that makes our country stronger and healthier and in the long run has the potential to reduce healthcare costs as well.

The fund is a substantial accomplishment, and we're very proud of that. And it's a great product of the Affordable Care Act. But when you put it next to the fact that treatment of chronic disease is contributing to over 75 percent of the $2.5 trillion in healthcare costs——

Senator ROBERTS. Doctor, I apologize for doing this, and I shouldn't. But I've got about 3 minutes here. And that was part of my opening comments, so I'm trying to buttress what you're saying in my opening comments.

Dr. KOH. Thank you.

Senator ROBERTS. But we get down to the details of the pragmatic use of the funds, and when you say proven prevention activities that you're funding, are there any of them that are experimental, or are they supported by scientific evidence? And that's going to be key if we're able to save the funds for what purpose they are intended.

So I don't expect you to list the whole laundry list of things that you are doing with State and local officials. But if you could be a little more specific on the pragmatic thing rather than—we all know that wellness is the way to go and prevention is the way to go if we're going to answer this question.

Dr. KOH. If we can take the example of tobacco, Senator, we know that tobacco dependence drives up cancer and heart disease and so many other conditions. We know that these are preventable illnesses. I'll give you the prime example. Lung cancer, which is primarily driven by tobacco dependence, is the leading cancer killer in our society. Without tobacco, that would be a rare condition, and it should be a rare condition.

Senator ROBERTS. OK. I'll use South Carolina as an example because the chairman brought it up. Specifically, what do you do with State and local officials to achieve this goal?

Dr. KOH. The South Carolina example the Senator mentioned was the Farm-to-School programs, where we're improving—or they're improving, actually, options for healthier foods for kids in schools so that those kids have a better chance of growing up with a healthy weight and not obese.

Senator ROBERTS. No. I want to know about tobacco. I don't smoke, by the way, but—only when I'm mad, Mr. Chairman. You know, specifically on——

Senator MIKULSKI. And there's evidence of that.

Senator ROBERTS. Yes, that's true.

[Laughter.]

She knows. At any rate, what is your yardstick to know that the programs and the fund really work? And specifically tobacco—other than just saying it's a heck of a problem. Yes, it is. It has been for years, but we are making some progress on it.

Dr. KOH. Sure.

Senator ROBERTS. Is there going to be scientific evidence, or is this experimental, or is it just advice and counsel, or what?

Dr. KOH. In areas like tobacco, the evidence is overwhelming.

Senator ROBERTS. No. In South Carolina, for the program, what happened?

Dr. KOH. Senator, I don't have the specifics on South Carolina tobacco control. But I can say in many States, the themes are the same, that is, improving cessation opportunities for smokers who want to quit, access to quit lines, making sure that public places are smoke-free so that workers aren't exposed to secondhand smoke in their work, education in schools so that kids don't get dependent in the first place, and really making this so-called Health In All Policies approach. And I'm sure that applies to South Carolina as just about every other State.

Senator ROBERTS. I'll leave it at that. I want to underscore, the kind of competition we have here in terms of funding for all the things we'd like to fund. And if you can't have a yardstick to know what programs actually have worked and get specific with our colleagues, we're going to have some problems.

Dr. KOH. Senator, if I can just add—for each of those components I mentioned, there are measureable yardsticks that get followed and tracked over time. So we can provide all that information for you.

Senator ROBERTS. I wish I had asked that first so he would have said that first, and then I could have gone to the next question. I'm sorry.

The CHAIRMAN. I have in order Senator Whitehouse, Senator Franken, Senator Mikulski.

Senator Whitehouse.

STATEMENT OF SENATOR WHITEHOUSE

Senator WHITEHOUSE. If I may, I'd like to followup on Senator Roberts' question. One can understand that, hypothetically or from past experience, a tobacco cessation program is, overall, a cost-benefit positive. But as we pursue the prevention effort and as we push out into other areas, it's going to be important to have a systematic, constant way of making the cost-benefit determination. And you will be a lot better off if we are all agreed that the numbers that you're working with are real numbers.

We have to work with CBO, and although we hate it, it adds a certain amount of order to the proceedings. What are the metrics for determining the cost justification for prevention plans right now? Do you have your own CBO? Do you have a shop where that gets done?

Dr. KOH. We depend on the Science Center, and we want to thank you for your commitment to getting good science and particularly through electronic health records and other ways——

Senator WHITEHOUSE. That's really not what I was getting at. I think—it sounds like you're telling us that there isn't a location within the Federal Government in which prevention strategies get formally evaluated as to their cost-benefit analysis and a rigorous and constant discipline is applied to those questions.

Dr. KOH. Those themes—I would disagree, actually, Senator. Those themes are aggressively pursued by agencies like NIH, like CDC and LSAR, Agency for Healthcare Research and Quality. And so the emphasis on scientific rigor, evaluation, accountability is very, very strong, and we——

Senator WHITEHOUSE. With respect to the cost-benefit equation?

Dr. KOH. Yes. We want to demonstrate return on investment, and we have some that, actually, Chairman Harkin recited with respect to vaccination return on investment and other areas.

Senator WHITEHOUSE. All right. Let me shift to a different topic and ask that I get a more complete—I think Senator Roberts may be interested in it as well—a more complete answer for the record, a written QFR on that point.

Dr. KOH. Sure.

Senator WHITEHOUSE. Because I think it would be helpful if, instead of sort of grabbing a cost-benefit analysis from here and another one from there and something that turned up in the literature somewhere else, you actually had your own program for determining what made the cuts, what didn't, what was the most cost benefit, what's the wisest place to deploy the funding that we have, and so forth.

That's my focus. I'm not challenging that you don't do this with any cost-benefit considerations being made. What I don't see is a place where this gets done consistently, reliably, by the same people, so you get a consistent body of expertise built up.

Dr. KOH. Actually, I can respond to that, Senator.

Senator WHITEHOUSE. I'd rather you not, because I have 2 minutes left. Do it in writing, OK, as I asked.

Dr. KOH. OK.

Senator WHITEHOUSE. Would that be all right?

Dr. KOH. Yes.

Senator WHITEHOUSE. What I'd like to use my last 2 minutes on is to urge you—as you know, you're standing in for the administration here. And so, I say this to everybody, so don't take it personally. But the prevention changes that we need to make in our healthcare system marry up with care coordination changes that we need to make as improvements to our healthcare system. And those marry up with quality reform improvements that we need to make in our healthcare system, and they marry up with payment reform improvements that we need to make to improve our healthcare system.

They all stand on electronic health infrastructure that needs to be the structure for evaluating and propagating all of those other missions that we have to accomplish. And I want to say again I am extremely frustrated that I see no apparent goal setting by the administration in this area. If you look at these things as not independent plans, but a strategy for delivery system reform that has these different components and that will reinforce one another—so you have to go forward globally with all of them.

You've got a great law in the Affordable Care Act in terms of the programs that were set up. You've got people like Don Berwick who are fantastic at this, and you've got them propagated throughout the administration. But what the administration has not yet done is to set a goal for itself as to what the end product of this exercise is going to be.

And I submit to you that the bureaucracy of this government would work a lot faster and a lot more effectively if it were working toward a specific, accountable outcome that the administration should announce. And I don't want to hear anybody tell me about bending the curve of healthcare costs. That is the most unaccountable metric you can imagine.

If President Kennedy, facing the space deficit that we had, had said he was going to bend the curve of space exploration, we would not have put a man on the moon and the speech would have been forgotten to history and justifiably so. And I want to just re-emphasize here my call on this administration—put a dollar figure and a date on the kind of savings you want to accomplish, describe how they're going to be done, and get the administration to work on those goals.

You cannot have the goals pursue the effort. You've got to have the goals lead the effort, and I don't see those goals.

Dr. KOH. If I can respond, Senator, I think I have a lot to share with you that will make you more supportive of what we're trying to do here. We have a national goal setting process called Healthy People, which you've probably heard about, that gets updated on a regular basis. We just updated Healthy People 2010 and put out Healthy People 2020 goals. And then the Affordable Care Act and the Prevention Fund helps us tremendously to reach those goals, Senator, because we are uniting both clinical prevention and community prevention.

There's an effort for a focus on community prevention services that look at return on investment issues, such as you've been talking about in your several questions to us. And there has been a national quality strategy that's been required by the Affordable Care Act that the department put out. Dr. Berwick was one of the co-authors along with Dr. Clancy of AHRQ.

With health IT in the middle of all that, we viewed this as a way of integrating all these efforts to reach those goals, make the country healthier, and, hopefully, make a difference on healthcare costs as well. So I would like to think that we're doing all the things you just described, Senator.

Senator WHITEHOUSE. I would like to also.

The CHAIRMAN. If I might just interject one thing, Dr. Koh, that there are two entities, one old and one new, I'd say to my friend, that—we have the U.S. Preventative Services Task Force, which has been in existence for a long time. They do look at cost benefits. They do look at science-based, evidence-based processes, and recommend those. So that's been there for some time.

18

We, in the Affordable Care Act, also set up the Prevention Council——

Dr. KOH. Yes.

The CHAIRMAN [continuing]. Where we have someone from 17 departments and agencies in the Federal Government. They are then supposed to look at proposals that cut across the entire Federal Government. I share your little frustration that they have been slow and haven't been too active, but we're going to look at that too. But that idea of being—what are the goals that cut across Department of Agriculture, Department of Defense, Department of Energy? What are the things that cut across all the departments? And that's what the Preventative Council is supposed to be doing.

Senator WHITEHOUSE. And what is the overall goal—would be my question—of the common exercise? How do you knit together the electronic health record piece, the various prevention councils, the quality reform efforts, the payment reform efforts? What goal are they together pointed at by the White House? That's what I can't determine.

The CHAIRMAN. I'd like to see that myself.

Dr. KOH. If I can respond to that, the overarching goals of Healthy People—again, which has been such a foundation for our work for 30 years—has been to improve quantity and quality of life, to eliminate health disparities, to——

The CHAIRMAN. Well, you do have some specific goals. I mentioned the Million Hearts Program, which is to reduce cardiovascular disease and strokes by how much, by a million?

Dr. KOH. By a million in 5 years.

The CHAIRMAN. In 5 years. So that's one goal they have, one goal, just on cardiovascular disease.

Dr. KOH. And if you want to get concrete on these initiatives, Mr. Chairman, another one that's received a lot of attention is Partnership for Patients, a goal to reduce hospital re-admissions and hospital-required conditions over the next several years. So these are programs where we try to merge our resources, make them efficient, effective, and make prevention really work.

The CHAIRMAN. And if I might just add one other thing, I'd say to my friend that in the past, so many times we've set up goals, and we never seem to achieve them. We set up this little goal and that little goal and this little goal.

I think what we tried to do in the Prevention Fund and the Affordable Care Act was to set up not so much a goal here and there and there, but to set up a dynamic, a system whereby there would be, as Dr. Koh said, this interrelationship between the clinical services, the community-based services, the workplace-based services, the school-based services that would all be working together in a dynamic to change the inputs into healthcare, so that over a period of time, you just have a different structure.

You have a different systems approach, rather than saying, "Well, we're going to work with everything we have, but we're going to have a goal." Well, if you work with everything you have and you have a goal, you're never going to get to the goal because the systems don't work. We have to change the systems. So I would just say that. But I agree that we do need goals out there, again, but still we need to change the system and not just have a goal for an unworkable system that we have now, I'd say to my friend.

Senator Franken.

STATEMENT OF SENATOR FRANKEN

Senator FRANKEN. Thank you, Mr. Chairman. I'd like to associate myself with the Senator from Rhode Island's remarks. We do want an overarching integration of all of the approaches that are being taken in the Affordable Care Act, because there are those of us who believe that this will save us tremendous amounts of money over the years and that we need to demonstrate that in a way that's convincing and in a way that's real.

And let me bore down into one thing that you write about in your testimony, which is the National Diabetes Prevention Program. You remember that I had you over a year ago come to my office?

Dr. KOH. Yes.

Senator FRANKEN. We had people from NIH and CDC, and we had United Health there. And this program started as an NIH clinical trial, became a CDC pilot, and it's the most evidence-based program to prevent the onset of Type 2 diabetes. I was proud to work with Senator Lugar and to include it in the healthcare reform.

Now, this program would cost $300 per individual. People who are pre-diabetic get 16 weeks of training in exercise at a Y, they get 16 weeks of nutritional training, and it reduces by 60 percent the number of pre-diabetics who became diabetic.

The significance of having United Healthcare, a private healthcare—the largest private healthcare insurer in the country—there was the woman from United Health who said, "We will cover anyone who's pre-diabetic that we're covering—we will pay for this program, and you know why? We will save $4 for every dollar." And I'd love for Senator Roberts to hear that, because this is a private healthcare company, a private health insurance company, saying, "We'll save $4 for every dollar."

Now, what I want to ask you is what would you say is the best way to scale this program up?

Dr. KOH. Well, Senator, first of all, thank you for a commitment to this area, because I can't think of a better example of evidence-based intervention than this one.

Senator FRANKEN. That's kind of why I brought it up. I just wanted to get specific and bore down into it. One detail thing—where United Health said, "We'll save $4 for every dollar we spend on this."

Dr. KOH. It's a great example of excellent science, of an intervention that makes a difference in the community. And we are committed to disseminating this across the country, as you are. A lot of this, of course, is constrained by resources, but it's also another great example of public-private partnerships in the role of the Y, and United Health Group has been extraordinary, as you mentioned.

I do have some figures in front of me that this effort is now available in some 44 cities across the country. Over 500 coaches have been trained to implement this with respect to people at high risk for diabetes. So it's one thing to gain evidence through excellent science, which has happened. It's another thing to disseminate them into the community and really make it come alive. So we're definitely on the second part of that right now.

Senator FRANKEN. I would just ask that you work with me to expand this program more broadly. Would you do that?

Dr. KOH. Absolutely.

Senator FRANKEN. Great. I wanted to go to one little piece of—I've only got a minute left, so this is more a comment, and then maybe you can respond a little bit. You write in your testimony,

"Good health also comes from clean air and water, safe outdoor spaces for physical activity, safe worksites, healthy foods, violence-free environments, and healthy homes."

And in your testimony you also talked about disparities in health, and I think nothing speaks to disparities in health more than that sentence, because there are people who don't have neighborhoods where there are outdoor spaces to run around. There are people who don't have clean air and clean water. There are people that don't have healthy foods, who live in violent communities.

We need to do something about the healthcare disparities in our country, and part of it can be in creating a society where people have that, which I think should be every kid's right to grow up in a neighborhood that will allow them to be healthy.

Dr. KOH. Thank you for a commitment to that. Environmental health and environmental justice is a key part of reducing disparities. And as you pointed out, Senator, health starts where people live, labor, learn, play, and pray. It's not just what happens to you in a doctor's office. So I completely agree with your sentiments. Thank you.

Senator FRANKEN. Thank you.

The CHAIRMAN. Senator Mikulski.

STATEMENT OF SENATOR MILKULSKI

Senator MIKULSKI. Thank you, Mr. Chairman.

Dr. Koh, we're just so glad to see you today and——

Dr. KOH. Thank you, Senator.

Senator MIKULSKI [continuing]. Thank you for all of your work. And what you have here are people who really believe in public health, have been strong advocates of prevention. And during the healthcare debate, Senator Kennedy established three task forces. One is on access to go over the rate of the number of people uninsured; one on prevention that Senator Harkin chaired and did a spectacular job. Many of the issues we're discussing today were Harkin initiatives, and I had the quality task force.

We found quality and prevention were intertwined. And it goes to Senator Whitehouse's comments about delivery systems and change there. And you know what? We just didn't want to change access, which was a big issue in our country, we wanted to be not only reformers, but we wanted to be transformers. And I think what you're hearing today—and I'm going to be part of this—is the rate of change and what are we doing that's transformational.

And as much as we like to hear about evidence-based, which we all support, the question is are we funding the status quo, are we funding the stagnant quo, or are we getting a sustained, synergistic effort that's transformative? And what do we mean? Public health and prevention has to have the elements of a social movement, that people take responsibility, they get help and assistance often outside of a doctor's office, and so on.

Often what we feel, with the implementation of this Affordable Care Act, is that the pace is slow. The White House Office of Personnel is notoriously sluggish, inert. We don't have all of our people in the Preventive Council. Senator Harkin and I put forth names. It took me 18 months to get one name through the White House in terms of the Preventive Health Council, in terms of the Advisory Council. So we're frustrated.

So what I would like to ask in my question to you is two things. First, what are you doing that's truly transformative and that we wouldn't have read in public health textbooks 10 years ago? The second thing is this preventive task force that Senator Harkin established so that every government agency would take ownership for what they did that would improve health outcomes for people.

Agriculture would be involved. Defense would be involved. We would learn from military medicine. Health would be involved. Education would be involved. Lisa Jackson—and they would all be coming together. Then we had an Advisory Council which we can't even get our names confirmed. So we're frustrated, sir.

Could you share with us kind of where you are, and could you shake up the Office of White House Personnel for us? That would be transformative.

[Laughter.]

Dr. KOH. Well, Senator, thank you for your commitment to a healthier society. We really respect and appreciate that. And you're absolutely right. This is a transformative opportunity, and I can give you the concrete examples you're asking for.

We've always funded prevention in Health and Human Services and in government for years, and you've been a leader at that. But establishing a dedicated fund, this Prevention Public Health Fund, gives us a rare opportunity to offer innovative new strategies, really step up commitment to prevention, really make a difference at the community level, and then do it in what we call a Health In All Policies approach, bringing in broad partners, non-traditional partners. So we could not do that without that fund. And so this is really an opportunity to do something really new and cutting edge at the community level.

The Health In All Policies approach is so key, because we are working with EPA—and you mentioned Administrator Jackson—with Housing, with Transportation. And this National Prevention Strategy that got unveiled a number of months ago by the Secretary—and Senator Harkin was at the unveiling—really celebrates having 17 Federal agencies working together on health. We often say that health is too important to be left to the health sector alone. And that's a new way of looking at health now than we ever had before.

So, Senator, I would like to think those opportunities are tremendous and, hopefully, will outweigh the frustrations of the day-to-day implementation. And I just want to thank you for your patience.

Senator MIKULSKI. What about the Advisory Council to the Preventive Council, to the council that's supposed to give us advice?

Dr. KOH. I'd be glad to get back to you on that. I had not heard the specifics on that. So I'd be pleased to do that. I am at HHS and not at the White House, so—but I'd be glad to get back to you.

Senator MIKULSKI. You know, that's what everybody says. They're not here, but they're going to be there. Believe me, you are a dedicated public servant and have dedicated your life to improving the health of people.

Dr. KOH. Thank you, Senator.

Senator MIKULSKI. But we've got to get this going, because there is doubt. People think this is a slush fund. The President himself wanted to cut it. We've got this window, and we have to show movement and momentum and the involvement of people. And I think otherwise, we're going to lose the opportunity.

Dr. KOH. Right. I really appreciate your commitment to this, Senator. No one wants to get this done faster than we do and I do. This is—and if I can say, Senator, and as I've mentioned, I've been waiting my whole life for an opportunity like this. And that's why to serve as the Assistant Secretary now, at this rare historic opportunity, is really indescribable, and we want to work closely with you and everybody to make prevention a reality in this country.

Senator MIKULSKI. Thank you.

The CHAIRMAN. I have to buttress what Senator Mikulski just said. When we get from OMB—and that's not your shop, that's the White House. When I get from OMB their suggestions for cutting this and shifting the monies, that doesn't set very well with us, who wanted to see this as transformative. I think Senator Mikulski has got the right word, transformative. And so we get a little frustrated with that.

Senator Roberts.

Senator ROBERTS. Mr. Chairman, I had no idea that the distinguished chairman of this committee and the distinguished Senator from Maryland was having so much trouble with the White House on appointments. It's been a very enlightening learning process for me. If it took 18 months for you to get back on one, think what would happen if that person was a Republican. It would have taken 24 months or something, or maybe 24 years, as the chairman has indicated.

Senator MIKULSKI. No. I think it would have happened faster.

Senator ROBERTS. OK. But the——

Senator MIKULSKI. It's different with you because of that smoking we talked about.

Senator ROBERTS. I'm disappointed that Senator Harkin did not associate himself with our remarks, Mr. Chairman. I merely opened the door and Sheldon beat it down. But I do want to work with the Senator, and I think we are on the same track. And I'll be very interested in that written response.

Let me give an example. Shawnee County, KS, is the home of Topeka, KS, the capital of Kansas. All of a sudden, there was a $1.2 million grant that sort of fell out of the sky to the Shawnee County Commission. That's outside of the Topeka city limits. And it was for educating senior citizens not to eat too much salt, or, as a matter of fact, not to eat any salt, but salt intake.

The county commissioners were not aware of this, but they said they surely could use the money. But they were advised that they had to use it for that particular program. Not to worry; there were quite a few groups that wanted to come to their assistance to do that.

But that's the kind of thing that I'm talking about that could really hurt us in regards to the objectives of what we all share. And to date, I still don't know the metrics of that. I still don't know what happened to the $1.2 million, and I still don't know how the Shawnee County Commission was going to have a program of outreach to senior citizens in the county.

Now, they hit the county because it's more rural, of course, in terms of access to professional healthcare providers. Obviously, your doctor is going to say, "Hey, you've got to watch your diet and get your blood pressure down," et cetera, et cetera. But I have yet to find out, how we're doing this.

Now, that's going to be sort of along the lines here that I was searching for in terms of a specific in these, as you say—you were much more specific in the Million Hearts initiative. I can't find my original commentary. But that's what I'm driving at. Would you care to comment? Because that could be $1.2 million that we could have used that, in other ways, would be more productive.

Dr. KOH. I would be happy to get you specifics on that particular grant, Senator. I don't know the specifics on that. But I can say, in general, that the grant awards are reviewed very carefully by independent committees. The competition for these awards is fierce. The Community Transformation Grant example I just mentioned that was unveiled by the CDC a couple of weeks ago—there were over 200 applications, and only 60 of those or so got funded, so less than one in three got funded.

And for each of them, they are heavily scored, and the measurement, the accountability, the outcomes, and the evaluation is what really is key, because we want to show at the end of these interventions that we've made a difference, how much it makes a difference, and then what the return on investment is, as Senator Whitehouse was asking about. So these are issues that we put into every grant review process, and the competition is very, very fierce.

Senator ROBERTS. I appreciate your response, and that's exactly the kind of thing that I think the Senator and I would like to have.

Dr. KOH. Thank you.

Senator ROBERTS. Thank you.

The CHAIRMAN. Thank you very much, Senator Roberts.

Senator Blumenthal. I recognize Senator Blumenthal.

STATEMENT OF SENATOR BLUMENTHAL

Senator BLUMENTHAL. Thank you, Mr. Chairman.

And thank you for being here, and thank you for your terrific work as a member of the administration and particularly on issues of prevention and, most particularly, in areas of tobacco prevention and cessation, which remains a really profoundly costly problem both in lives and dollars for our society. And I appreciate the change in approach and attitude of this administration as compared with previous ones, and that is due largely to your leadership. So I commend and thank you.

And in that connection, could you perhaps update us if you have information about the so-called deeming regulation, what its current status is within the FDA, if you know?

Dr. KOH. I'm sorry, Senator. The term again?

Senator BLUMENTHAL. The deeming regulation that, in effect, applies to tobacco control activities of the FDA. And if you're not familiar with it, I'll move on.

Dr. KOH. OK. Senator, I'm not familiar with the term. I can say, as you well know, the FDA has created a new Center for Tobacco Products. They are committed to implementing the new law that was signed by the President in June 2009. There are a number of regulatory activities that are proceeding forward, mostly to protect kids. New graphic warning labels have been proposed for cigarettes to hit the market in the fall of next year.

Through those efforts, we are asking all organizations that have anything to do with tobacco, its manufacturing, its distribution, its sale to be registered with the FDA Center for Tobacco Products, and that has been completed. So these are, again, historic efforts that we hope will make tobacco control come alive. You know better than anyone, Senator, because you've been such a leader, that the tobacco successes in terms of reducing dependence has stalled in the last number of years. And we need to make a difference now, and we want to use this opportunity to get there.

Again, the Affordable Care Act and the Prevention Fund has had dedicated funds for tobacco control efforts at the community level. So have these so-called Community Transformation Grants. So there are many, many ways we're trying to tackle this. And this is all an area where there's overwhelming evidence about what works. This is all evidence-based, science-driven efforts, and the challenge has been we have not been able to disseminate it and really make it come alive. So we hope that this is our opportunity to do so.

Senator BLUMENTHAL. And just so perhaps we have you on record, what would you say works best in this area?

Dr. KOH. Well, it's a multi-pronged strategy to, obviously, raise awareness and educate the public, especially young people; to offer cessation services through quit lines and other efforts; to promote the use of effective pharmaceutical interventions when appropriate; raising the price has an effect on lowering consumption; increasing smoke-free workplaces to create a new social norm for tobacco. So these are all efforts to create a healthier, tobacco-free society.

Senator BLUMENTHAL. And in terms of cessation and the quit line, has it been your experience—I think there's evidence for it— that the best approach is really combined counseling, pharmaceutical drug assistance, a sort of multifaceted approach, rather than just relying on one or another?

Dr. KOH. Absolutely, Senator. We often stress in public health that there's often not one magic bullet but multiple ways of addressing problems that work together. And particularly in tobacco, we need counseling, we need outreach, we need education, and then creating a new norm, so to predict the next generation. Those are all elements that work together in this critical field.

Senator BLUMENTHAL. And that fact applies to Medicaid and Medicare patients as well as others.

Dr. KOH. Especially to Medicaid patients and Medicare patients. And you know so well, Senator, that the smoking rates in Medicaid populations is close to twice what it is in the general population. So we need special attention there. And if I can say to both you and the chairman that we have some evidence in Medicaid interventions at the statewide level that really improving outreach and cessation can make a difference in terms of reducing prevalence and then saving money as well. So that's very promising evidence-based work that can be active prevention and also save money at the same time.

Senator BLUMENTHAL. Thank you. And thank you for your very important work in this area.

Dr. KOH. Thank you, Senator.

The CHAIRMAN. Dr. Koh, Secretary Koh, thank you very, very much, unless you had some closing thing that you wanted to say.

Dr. KOH. We can followup with Senator Blumenthal on the deeming regulation. I have heard it as substantial equivalents. That's the term that I had in my head. So there are regulations to deem non-cigarettes as tobacco products so the FDA can regulate them. And the so-called substantial equivalents effort that's ongoing—we can get you more information on that.

Senator BLUMENTHAL. Thank you.

The CHAIRMAN. Thank you very much.

Dr. KOH. Thank you, Mr. Chairman.

The CHAIRMAN. Thanks for being here.

Now we'll move to our second panel. I will introduce them as they come up to the table. First, we welcome Ms. Nancy Brown. Ms. Brown is the chief executive officer of the American Heart Association. As the CEO, Ms. Brown leads the AHA in continuing their work as the world's largest voluntary health organization dedicated to preventing, treating, and defeating cardiovascular diseases and stroke.

We also have Dr. John Seffrin. Dr. Seffrin is the chief executive officer of the American Cancer Society. Under his leadership, the society has become the largest health organization fighting cancer with significant resources to help develop early detection methods and find cures. Dr. Seffrin currently serves on the Advisory Group on Prevention, Health Promotion, and Integrative and Public Health that is responsible for advising the National Prevention Council on prevention and health promotion. Those were established by the Affordable Care Act.

Next we have Mr. John Griffin, Jr., chair of the board of the American Diabetes Association, the Nation's largest organization leading the fight to stop diabetes. Mr. Griffin has a wealth of legal experience in diabetes as he serves on the board of directors and chairs the Legal Advocacy Subcommittee for the ADA. He serves on the Texas Diabetes Council by appointment of the Governor of Texas and is managing partner of his law firm in Victoria, TX. That's near Beeville, TX. How would I know about Beeville, TX? I went through flight training there.

And Dr. Tevi Troy, our final witness, Senior Fellow at the Hudson Institute. In his capacity, Dr. Troy consults on healthcare and other domestic economic policy issues. Prior to his position at Hudson, he served as the Deputy Secretary of the Department of

Health and Human Services from 2007 to 2009, and also directed the White House Domestic Policy Council under President George W. Bush.

Thank you for being here today, Dr. Troy.

Again, all of your statements will be made a part of the record in their entirety. I ask—in order of introduction, we'll just go from left to right—if you could sum up in 5 minutes or so, we'd appreciate it so we can get into a dialogue.

Ms. Brown, welcome and please proceed.

STATEMENT OF NANCY BROWN, CHIEF EXECUTIVE OFFICER, AMERICAN HEART ASSOCIATION, DALLAS, TX

Ms. BROWN. Thank you, Mr. Chairman and Senator Roberts. I want to thank you for this opportunity to discuss the importance of prevention in the fight against cardiovascular diseases and stroke.

Cardiovascular diseases are the deadliest and most prevalent illnesses in our Nation. More than 82 million adults in the United States have been diagnosed with some form of cardiovascular disease and someone dies from it every 39 seconds. Along with the enormous physical and emotional toll cardiovascular disease exacts, it is also America's costliest illness, accounting for 17 percent of overall health expenditures.

The direct medical costs of treating cardiovascular diseases are estimated at $273 billion in 2010, and the annual indirect costs, including lost productivity, come to $172 billion. All in all, that adds up to $445 billion. The future looks even worse. We project that by 2030, two out of five Americans, or 116 million people, or 40 percent of the population, will have some form of cardiovascular disease. The associated costs are staggering. Total direct and nondirect costs are expected to exceed a whopping $1 trillion by the year 2030.

However, there's hope in what could be characterized as a sea change in how we view this deadly disease. Despite being the No. 1 killer of all Americans, research has demonstrated that cardiovascular disease is largely preventable. A report in the *New England Journal of Medicine* found that 67 percent of the decline in heart disease death rates in the United States between 1980 and 2000 was due to reductions in cholesterol, blood pressure, smoking, and physical inactivity. And to the surprise of many, only about 7 percent was the result of bypass surgery or angioplasty.

Prevention holds the key to changing the trajectory of these projections if we're willing to take deliberate and focused actions to prevent or delay the many forms of cardiovascular disease. Studies estimate that people who reach middle age with optimal cardiovascular health have only a 6 to 8 percent chance of developing cardiovascular disease in their lifetime. And as I sit here today, although 39 percent of all Americans believe they're in ideal cardiovascular health, actually fewer than 1 percent are.

To do this, we must reorient our entire national approach to promote healthy habits and wellness at an early age. We must reach individuals before they actually become patients, suffering a heart attack or any other acute cardiovascular event. We have to get in the game earlier to influence the final score and make a positive difference in people's lives.

We believe at the American Heart Association that we must take a two-pronged prevention approach: first, what has been referred to as primordial prevention and, second, primary prevention. Both public and private prevention initiatives present the largest opportunities to make a positive impact on our Nation's physical and fiscal health, national security, and workforce productivity. And research demonstrates that some interventions can have a major impact on improving public health and saving precious taxpayer dollars.

We have a paper published in circulation in July of this year that provides the background for some of these statistics I'm about to give you. For example, research in Massachusetts showed that comprehensive coverage of tobacco cessation services in the Medicaid program led to reduced hospitalizations for heart attacks and a net savings of $10.5 million or a $3.07 return on investment for every dollar spent in the first 2 years.

Comprehensive smoke-free air laws in public buildings bring an estimated $10 billion in annual savings for direct and indirect healthcare costs. And community-based programs to increase physical activity, improve nutrition, and prevent smoking show a return on investment of $5.60 for every dollar spent within 5 years.

So why, then, might you ask, is prevention taking a back seat to acute care and treatment? There are many complex reasons for this and environmental barriers to overcome that I discuss in my written testimony, but one overarching issue I'd like to focus on. Like all pressing problems facing our Nation today, there must be a shared responsibility when it comes to preventing cardiovascular disease. That includes individuals themselves, our government, and not-for-profit organizations like the American Heart Association.

First of all, individuals must take more responsibility for their health through lifestyle changes, such as eating better, exercising, and not smoking. Unfortunately, we know from our own research a vast majority of Americans are not in optimal cardiovascular health, as I mentioned before, although 39 percent of them believe that they are.

Government can help by supporting policies that promote an environment more conducive to positive health, encourage healthier lifestyles, and reward businesses, healthcare providers, and communities that provide quality preventative care and healthier environments.

And we at the American Heart Association will continue to promote awareness in the public and medical communities of the need and importance of prevention. We'll also continue to support research aimed at identifying new and better ways to prevent the onset of cardiovascular disease and support volunteer-led programs throughout the country that put this knowledge into action. We will engage people as activists in their own health, and we will continue to implement quality improvement programs like the American Heart Association's Get with the Guidelines program which has documented more lives saved and lower healthcare costs in this country.

Thank you for the opportunity to present this information today, and at the appropriate time, I'd be happy to answer any questions. [The prepared statement of Ms. Brown follows:]

PREPARED STATEMENT OF NANCY BROWN

SUMMARY

Mr. Chairman, I want to thank you for this opportunity to discuss the importance of prevention in the fight against cardiovascular diseases and stroke. Cardiovascular diseases are the deadliest and most prevalent illness in our Nation. More than 82 million adults in the United States have been diagnosed with some form of cardiovascular disease, and someone dies from it every 39 seconds.

Along with the enormous physical and emotional toll cardiovascular disease exacts, it is also America's costliest illness, accounting for 17 percent of overall health expenditures. The direct medical costs of treating cardiovascular disease are estimated at $273 billion in 2010. The annual indirect costs, which refer to lost productivity, come to $172 billion. All in all, that adds up to $444 billion.

The future bodes even worse. We project that by 2030 two out of five Americans—116 million people, or 40 percent of the population—will have some form of cardiovascular disease. The associated costs are staggering. Total direct and non-direct costs are expected to exceed a whopping $1 trillion.

However, there is hope in what could be characterized as a sea change in how we view this deadly disease. Despite being the No. 1 killer of all Americans, research has demonstrated that cardiovascular disease is largely preventable. A report in the *New England Journal of Medicine* found that 67 percent of the decline in heart disease death rates in the United States between 1980 and 2000 was due to reductions in cholesterol, blood pressure, smoking and physical inactivity—and to the surprise of many—only about 7 percent was the result of bypass surgery or angioplasty.

Indeed, prevention holds the key to changing the trajectory of these projections if we are willing to take deliberate and focused actions to prevent or delay the many forms of cardiovascular disease. Studies estimate that people who reach middle age with optimal cardiovascular health have only a 6 to 8 percent chance of developing cardiovascular disease in their lifetime.

But to do so we must reorient our entire national approach to promote healthy habits and wellness at an early age. We must reach individuals before they actually become "patients" suffering a heart attack or any other acute cardiovascular event. Let me put it a different way. We have to get into the game earlier to influence the final score and make a positive difference in people's lives.

We must take a two-pronged prevention approach. First, what has been referred to as "primordial" prevention, which prevents the development of risk factors.

Second is "primary" prevention which consists of interventions to reduce worrisome risk factors like high blood pressure or high cholesterol once they're present, with the goal of preventing an initial acute event.

Both public and private prevention initiatives present the largest opportunities to make a positive impact on our Nation's physical and fiscal health, national security, and workforce productivity. And research demonstrates that some interventions can have a major impact on improving public health and saving precious taxpayer dollars. For example:

• Research in Massachusetts showed that comprehensive coverage of tobacco cessation services in the Medicaid program led to reduced hospitalizations for heart attacks and a net savings of $10.5 million or a $3.07 return on investment for every dollar spent in the first 2 years.

• Comprehensive smoke-free air laws in public buildings bring an estimated $10 billion in annual savings for direct and indirect healthcare costs.

• Community-based programs to increase physical activity improve nutrition and prevent smoking use show a return on investment of $5.60 for every dollar spent within 5 years.

So why is prevention taking a back seat to acute care and treatment? There are many complex reasons and environmental barriers to overcome that I discuss in my written testimony. But let me focus on the overarching issue.

Like all of the pressing problems confronting our Nation today, there must be a shared responsibility when it comes to preventing cardiovascular disease. That includes individuals, government, and non-profits, such as the American Heart Association.

Individuals must take more responsibility for their health through lifestyle changes, such as eating better, exercising, and not smoking. Unfortunately we know from our own research that a vast majority of Americans are not in optimal cardiovascular health—although nearly 40 percent believe that they are.

Government can help by supporting policies that promote an environment more conducive to positive health, encourage healthier lifestyles and reward businesses, health care providers, and communities that provide quality preventative care and healthy environments.

And we at the American Heart Association will continue to promote awareness in both the public and medical communities of the need and importance of prevention. We will also continue to support research aimed at identifying new and better ways to prevent the onset of cardiovascular disease and support volunteer-run programs throughout the country that put this knowledge into practice. Our organization has embraced an ambitious 2020 goal to improve the cardiovascular health of all Americans and reduce deaths from cardiovascular diseases and stroke by 20 percent.

But we can't do this alone—the problem is too large for any one group to accomplish. The only way we can solve this problem is by working together and we look forward to that opportunity.

I would be happy to answer any questions.

_____

INTRODUCTION

Chairman Harkin, Ranking Member Enzi and members of the committee, I want to thank you for this opportunity to present the American Heart Association's research and views on the importance of prevention in the fight against cardiovascular diseases and stroke. Cardiovascular disease (CVD) is the deadliest and most prevalent illness in our Nation. More than 82 million adults in the United States have been diagnosed with some form of cardiovascular disease, and someone dies from it every 39 seconds.

Along with the enormous physical and emotional toll cardiovascular disease exacts, it is also America's costliest illness, accounting for 17 percent of overall health expenditures. According to a recent American Heart Association article/policy statement, "Value of Primordial and Primary Prevention for Cardiovascular Disease" published in our journal *Circulation* (*http://circ.ahajournals.org/content/124/8/967.full.pdf+html?sid=2ea4c775-5912-4cf8-8c42-13ab84042e2f*), the direct medical costs of treating cardiovascular disease are estimated at $273 billion in 2010. The annual indirect costs, which refer to lost productivity, come to $172 billion. All in all, that adds up to $445 billion.

The future bodes even worse. We project that by 2030 two out of five Americans—116 million people, or 40 percent of the population—will have some form of cardiovascular disease. The associated costs are staggering. Total direct and non-direct costs are expected to exceed a whopping $1 trillion making this a critical medical and societal issue.

A SEA CHANGE

However, there is hope in what could be characterized as a sea change in how we view this deadly disease. Despite being the No. 1 killer of all Americans, research has demonstrated that cardiovascular disease is largely preventable.

Indeed, we can change the trajectory of these frightening projections if we as a nation are willing to take deliberate and focused actions to prevent or delay the many forms of cardiovascular disease. The facts speak for themselves and let me cite some of the more prominent ones.

Studies estimate that people who reach middle age with optimal risk levels have only a 6 to 8 percent chance of developing cardiovascular disease in their lifetime.

It is estimated that if all Americans had access to recommended CVD prevention activities, myocardial infarctions and strokes would be reduced by 63 percent and 31 percent respectively in the next 30 years.

Men and women who lower their risk factors may have 79–82 percent fewer heart attacks and strokes than those who do not reduce their risk factors.

A recent review by the U.S. Preventive Services Task Force showed that counseling to improve diet or increase physical activity changed health behaviors and was associated with small improvements in weight, blood pressure, and cholesterol levels.

And this is perhaps the most telling statistic of all. Approximately 67 percent of the decline in U.S. age-adjusted coronary heart disease death rates from 1980–2000 can be attributed to improvements in risk factors including reductions in total blood cholesterol, systolic blood pressure, smoking prevalence, and physical inactivity—only about 7 percent was the result of bypass surgery or angioplasty. However, these reductions were partially offset by increases in the prevalence of obesity. It is much more difficult and costly to reverse obesity and diabetes once they occur than to prevent them from developing in the first place.

SETTING THE STAGE FOR TRANSFORMATION

We as a nation must reorient our entire approach to promote healthy habits and wellness at an early age. We must transform the current healthcare delivery system that focuses on "sick care" to one that better incorporates, coordinates, values and financially rewards quality and prevention.

We must reach individuals before they actually become "patients" suffering a heart attack or any other acute cardiovascular event. Let me put it a different way. We have to get into the game earlier to influence the final score and make a positive difference in people's lives.

We must take a two-pronged prevention approach. First is "primordial" prevention, which prevents the development of risk factors.

Second is "primary" prevention which consists of interventions to modify adverse risk factors once they're present, with the goal of preventing an initial acute event.

To this end, the American Heart Association created "Life's Simple 7", which are seven key modifiable health factors and behaviors that we believe are essential for successful prevention of cardiovascular disease. They include regular physical activity, a heart healthy diet, no smoking, weight management and control of blood pressure, cholesterol and blood sugar. These are literally lessons for life.

A SOLID RETURN ON INVESTMENT

These and other public and private prevention initiatives present the best opportunities to make a positive impact on our Nation's physical and fiscal health. In a time of tight budgets and limited resources when the Administration and Congress are looking for a solid return on investments, prevention is a proven winner.

Research already demonstrates that environment and policy change can have a major impact on improving public health and saving precious taxpayer dollars. For example, research in Massachusetts showed that comprehensive coverage of tobacco cessation services in the Medicaid program led to reduced hospitalizations for heart attacks and a net savings of $10.5 million or a $3.07 return on investment for every dollar spent in the first 2 years.

Community-based programs to increase physical activity, improve nutrition, and prevent smoking and other tobacco use can show a return on investment of $5.60 for every dollar spent within 5 years.

Moreover, comprehensive worksite wellness programs can lower medical costs by approximately $3.27 and absenteeism costs by about $2.73 in the first 12 to 18 months for every dollar spent.

And speaking of getting into the game earlier, robust school-based initiatives to promote healthy eating and physical activity have shown a cost effectiveness of $900–$4,305 per quality-of-life-year saved.

MILLION HEARTS INITIATIVE

One other reason to be optimistic about the potential for a heightened focus on prevention is the Department of Health and Human Services' recently announced Million Hearts Initiative (Million Hearts).

This new initiative will focus, coordinate, and enhance CVD prevention in programs and activities across all HHS agencies with the aggressive goal of preventing 1 million heart attacks and strokes over the next 5 years (by 2016).

By pledging to partner with and work alongside healthcare providers, nonprofit organizations, and the private sector, Million Hearts represents an unprecedented commitment on the part of Secretary Sebelius and the HHS to make preventing heart attacks and stroke a top national health priority.

The American Heart Association not only applauds the launch of Million Hearts but also is grateful for the opportunities we have been provided to help inform, shape, and support the initiative. We look forward to joining and partnering with Secretary Sebelius and the HHS in implementing this initiative, which has the potential to advance the mission and work of the American Heart Association dramatically and to help us achieve our ambitious "Impact Goal" to improve the cardiovascular health of all Americans and reduce deaths from cardiovascular diseases and stroke by 20 percent by 2020.

Million Hearts represents a bold opportunity to bring CVD prevention to the forefront of Federal healthcare policy. As the leading voluntary health organization in the field of CVD, the American Heart Association is committed to this initiative and welcomes an opportunity to take a leadership role in its implementation.

In addition to working to help inform and shape the Million Hearts initiative, the American Heart Association is prepared to partner with the Centers for Disease Control and Prevention and other HHS agencies on various activities, and is also committed to working with HHS to hold ourselves collectively accountable for achieving its goals. This includes evaluating and publicly reporting progress toward reducing 1 million heart attacks and strokes over the next 5 years. The Guideline Advantage program—a jointly directed quality improvement program from the American Cancer Society, the American Diabetes Association and the American Heart Association—may help contribute to these surveillance efforts. This program works with practices' existing EHR or health technology platform to extract relevant patient data and quarterly reports, and benchmarking on adherence to guidelines.

In addition to improving CVD prevention in the next 5 years, Million Hearts aims to use the prevention of CVD as a model for how health reform can work to make a dramatic, immediate, and sustainable impact on the healthcare system to save lives and to prevent chronic disease. The lessons learned from Million Hearts will inform complementary implementation efforts addressing other chronic conditions.

THE STATE OF PREVENTION TODAY

We are starting to place a greater emphasis on prevention. However, we still have a long way to go to "walk the talk" as access to and use of preventive services remain stubbornly low.

Indeed, let me share with the committee some very informative and alarming statistics about CVD preventable risk factors and where we stand today. They are clearly a call to greater action; millions of lives are at risk.

There are tremendous gaps in clinical prevention: only 47 percent of patients at increased risk of CVD are prescribed aspirin; one in three Americans have high blood pressure, however, only 46 percent of them have it adequately controlled; only 33 percent of people with high cholesterol have adequately controlled low-density lipoprotein cholesterol; and just 26 percent of those who want to quit smoking receive adequate support services.

In addition, effective community prevention interventions, such as eliminating exposure to secondhand smoke and decreasing sodium and *trans* fat intake in the population, have been underused because of a lack of a coordinated national effort to make these population interventions available to reduce CVD.

Only 18 percent of U.S. adults follow three important measures recommended by the American Heart Association for optimal health: not smoking, maintaining a healthy body weight, and exercising at moderate-vigorous intensity for at least 30 minutes, 5 days per week.

In 2009, adult obesity rates rose in 28 States and in more than two-thirds of States, more than 25 percent of all adults are obese.

The number of overweight pre-schoolers jumped 36 percent since 1999–2000. Nearly 1 of every 6 children and adolescents ages 2–19 are considered obese. Sadly, one study has shown that obese children's arteries resemble those of a middle-aged adult.

The percentage of high school students who smoke decreased over 34 percent from 1999 to 2009. Still, over 3,800 children under 18 try a cigarette for the first time each day. An estimated 6.4 million of them can be expected to die prematurely as a result.

A sedentary lifestyle contributes to coronary heart disease. However, moderate-intensity physical activity, such as brisk walking, is associated with a substantial reduction in chronic disease. It is estimated that $5.6 billion in heart disease costs could be saved if 10 percent of Americans began a regular walking program. Still, 33 percent of U.S. adults report that they do not do any vigorous physical activity.

At least 65 percent of people with Type 2 diabetes die from some form of heart disease or stroke. Unfortunately, diabetes prevalence increased 90 percent from 1995–1997 to 2005–2007 in the 33 States that tracked data for both time periods.

About 25.4 million American adults have diagnosed or undiagnosed diabetes and the prevalence of pre-diabetes in the adult population is nearly 37 percent. Diabetes disproportionately affects Hispanics, blacks, Native Americans and Alaskan Natives.

Approximately 44 percent of U.S. adults have unhealthy total cholesterol levels of 200 mg/dL or higher. A 10-percent decrease in total blood cholesterol levels population-wide may result in an estimated 30 percent reduction in the incidence of CHD. Unfortunately, fewer than half of the people who qualify for cholesterol lowering treatment are receiving it.

If these statistics were not troubling enough, according to a new Commonwealth Fund-supported study in the journal *Health Policy*, the United States ranks last among 16 high-income industrialized Nations when it comes to deaths that could potentially have been prevented with timely access to effective health care. That is not a distinction we should be proud of as a nation.

WHAT WE HAVE LEARNED SO FAR

Although we are still in the early stages of the transformation from "sick care" to preventive care, we have already learned some valuable lessons that can help guide our future individual and collective efforts.

Policy change makes the greatest impact when it optimizes the environments where people live, learn, work and play—offices, schools, homes, and communities, making healthier behaviors and healthier choices the norm by default or by design, putting individual behavior in the context of multiple-level influences.

Research continues to demonstrate that environment and policy change have some of the greatest impact in improving public health, providing the counter argument to those policymakers who argue that government has no role, that health is determined solely by individual responsibility.

Although there may not be significant cost-savings in the short-term to society there is value in making an important investment in the long-term health of our Nation.

The medical and research communities are challenged to further clarify the effectiveness and sustainability of cost-effective preventive cardiovascular services so that proven interventions can be provided in home-, work-, school- and community-based settings to save lives, money, and resources.

Finally, legislators, public health and planning professionals and community representatives can help to facilitate this objective by empowering localities to embrace a culture of lifestyle that incorporates physical activity, healthy nutrition options, smoking bans, and affordable access to health care for all Americans.

WHAT IS HOLDING US BACK?

All of these findings and lessons learned beg the questions, "Why is prevention taking a back seat to acute care and treatment? Why aren't more efforts and dollars being spent on prevention?" The answers are not easy and there are many barriers to overcome to get to the solutions.

First, prevention is a long-term commitment; policymakers are generally focused on a much shorter timeframe with tangible benefits delivered in the near term.

Second, as a Nation, we have made a significant investment in acute care and treatment which is much more impressive than prevention efforts. Treatments like open heart surgery have the "wow" factor that prevention lacks.

Third, the line of sight between preventive actions and results is significantly longer and harder to reinforce. If a patient is admitted with chest pains, a diagnosis is made and appropriate treatment is started—usually that same day.

However, if someone who is overweight sees their doctor and loses weight, the positive results of that weight loss may not be evident for months, years or even decades later and may exhibit in less "obvious" ways such as reduced absenteeism from work.

And finally, prevention's attribute as a cost-saver has created the unintended situation where it is necessary to justify spending resources to prevent disease when we do not have to justify funding focused on treating conditions that could have been prevented.

For these reasons, and others, prevention is ironically still an afterthought to acute care and treatment. This is all backwards because if you look at what's moving the needle and improving health, it is prevention efforts.

Indeed, the only way to truly reduce healthcare costs in this country is to have a healthier American population which will only come if we can improve the health and health status through prevention.

There are certainly many other complex reasons and environmental hurdles to overcome in the transformation to preventive healthcare and ultimately a healthier and more productive society, but let me focus on the overarching issue.

Like all of the pressing problems confronting our Nation today, there must be a shared responsibility when it comes to preventing cardiovascular disease. That includes individuals, government, and non-profits, such as the American Heart Association, the American Diabetes Association, and the American Cancer Society.

Individuals must take responsibility for their health through lifestyle changes, such as eating better, exercising, and not smoking. Government can help provide the tools to help them meet these goals, such as incentives for businesses to create healthy work environments and funding to test for risk factors.

And we at the American Heart Association will continue our role to promote awareness in both the public and medical communities of the need and importance of prevention. We will also continue to support research aimed at identifying new and better ways to prevent the onset of cardiovascular disease and support volunteer-run programs throughout the country that put this knowledge into practice. In other words, we are all in this together and the only way we can solve this problem is by working together.

I would be happy to answer any questions.

The CHAIRMAN. Thank you, Ms. Brown.

Dr. Seffrin, welcome back to the committee. You've been here before.

Mr. SEFFRIN. I have, Senator Harkin. Thank you. And by the way, on behalf of the American Cancer Society—as part of the record—you've been officially forgiven for taking Dan Smith away from us.

[Laughter.]

The CHAIRMAN. And don't come trying to get him back, either.

STATEMENT OF JOHN R. SEFFRIN, Ph.D., CHIEF EXECUTIVE OFFICER, AMERICAN CANCER SOCIETY, ATLANTA, GA

Mr. SEFFRIN. Senator Harkin and Senator Roberts, I want to summarize my formal written testimony in just a few words of saying what do we know, what do we know for sure, and what do we know works? And what we know is that the No. 1 health, disease, and disability challenge of the 21st Century for America will be non-communicable diseases, chronic disease—not second, not third, No. 1. We know that to be the case.

We are faced with a virtual tsunami of chronic disease if we don't intervene. If we knew when the next real tsunami would hit, and we knew what to do about it and didn't do anything, I would suggest we'd passed up a moral imperative to act. So when it comes to non-communicable diseases, like cancer and heart disease and diabetes and others, if we're really serious about reducing human suffering and premature death from cancer and other NCDs and, over time, reducing overall healthcare costs, we have to understand four things.

No. 1, prevention is the best policy. No. 2, prevention is the best buy. No. 3, prevention is the best cure. And No. 4, prevention is best for the economy of America and, indeed, the world. A word or two about each of those.

First, Prevention is the best policy because it works. Prevention works as Dr. Koh said it works. We are saving 350 more lives each and every day from cancer today than we were in 1991 when Dan came to work for us—350 per day more than we were saving then. The lion's share of that is from effective prevention interventions—people either not starting to smoke or being able to quit or get the proper screening they need.

Second, prevention is the best buy. We now have good documentation that the prevention efforts that work, the interventions that work to forestall or to prevent chronic disease can be implemented from $1 to $3 per person per year—not a bad buy, it would seem to me.

Third, prevention is the best cure. One of the things a lot of people don't realize is that of the 1.4 million Americans who were diagnosed with cancer this year, 60 percent of them could have been prevented with what we already know to do today. A third would disappear almost overnight if we just got rid of tobacco.

Fourth, prevention is the best for the economy. To give you some sense of the proportionality, the global cost of cancer is $895 billion per year, three times as much as HIV/AIDS and tuberculosis and malaria combined. And yet, interestingly, cancer isn't on the G–8 health agenda, the G–20 health agenda, and so forth.

Or let me explain it a different way. If we choose not to intervene, globally, in the next 20 years, we will have lost economic output of $47 trillion globally—lost economic—I'm not talking about the healthcare cost of treating sick people or disabled. I'm talking about the economic lost productivity—$47 trillion. That's more money than I can conceptualize, so I'll put it this way. That's 75 percent of the global GDP in 2010. Or put still another way, it's enough money to eliminate $2 a day poverty to the 2.5 billion inhabitants of planet earth that are on $2 a day poverty for a century.

So let me just sum up by saying I think it's extremely important for Americans to better understand, but especially policymakers to understand that unless we make prevention the centerpiece of our healthcare system, we're going to miss an opportunity to become the healthiest Nation. Prevention is the best cure.

[The prepared statement of Dr. Seffrin follows:]

PREPARED STATEMENT OF JOHN R. SEFFRIN, PH.D.

SUMMARY

We are facing a tsunami of chronic disease in this century. Cancer and other noncommunicable diseases (NCDs) represent a new frontier in the fight to improve our Nation's health. While we have made great strides over the past two decades in reducing the rate of death from cancer, we are in danger of falling behind previous generations. Although we have cut in half the percentage of regular tobacco users, 20 percent of the population still smokes, and the rate of childhood obesity due to bad diet and lack of physical activity has reached epidemic proportions. For the first time in our Nation's history our children could on average live shorter lives than their parents.

We know that half of cancer deaths are preventable. Much of the suffering and death from cancer that occurs today, and the substantial cost we incur of treating advanced disease, could be reduced through evidence-based prevention. That means more systematic efforts to reduce tobacco use, improve diet and physical activity, reduce obesity, develop and deliver preventive vaccines, and expand the use of established early detection screening tests.

It is important to note that throughout history prevention has been the key to bringing known diseases under control. It has been prevention in the public health sphere that has virtually eliminated epidemics of plague, cholera, yellow fever, measles and polio from our shores. This is what we need to do to prevent the next epidemic of cancer, heart disease and diabetes. We must go on the attack against childhood obesity and tobacco use and other causes of these diseases now or we will be overwhelmed by the cost of treating them later. Spending on prevention, particularly in the area of cancer, is an important down payment to improve the health of our communities and families. But we still need to do more.

Today, we know more about cancer than ever before, but while we continue to make important progress, we have not yet realized the true potential we already have to save lives and reduce suffering from this terrible disease. The simple truth is that while more Americans were saved from cancer last year than ever before, it is also true that millions of Americans still suffer and die from cancer. It doesn't have to be this way.

We don't need a magic bullet to control cancer, what we need is the will and courage to do the right things. If we do, we can and will significantly hasten the day when cancer is no longer a significant public health threat in America and around the world.

———

Good afternoon, Mr. Chairman, Senator Enzi, and distinguished members of the committee. Thank you for the opportunity to testify today about the importance of prevention. I am Dr. John Seffrin, chief executive officer of the American Cancer Society (the Society) and the American Cancer Society Cancer Action Network (ACS CAN). On behalf of the millions of cancer patients and survivors in America today, I want to thank you for holding this hearing and for your continued leadership in the fight against cancer.

THE BURDEN OF CANCER IN AMERICA AND WORLDWIDE

Cancer and other non-communicable diseases (NCDs) represent a new frontier in the fight to improve global health. Because of rising incidence rates worldwide, NCDs are now responsible for more deaths than all other causes combined. In 2008, 36 million people died from NCDs, representing 63 percent of the 57 million global deaths that year. By 2030, deaths from NCDs are projected to grow to 52 million people each year.[1] This epidemic is fueled by a combination of growing risk factors, including continued tobacco use, unhealthy diets, and insufficient physical activity. NCDs pose obvious harm to families and communities as individuals get sick and die but they are also an increasing drag on the U.S. economy and on economies worldwide. Recent research from Harvard University suggests a cumulative economic output loss of $47 trillion over the next two decades from cardiovascular disease, chronic respiratory disease, cancer, diabetes and untreated mental health illnesses.[1]

In the United States this year, cancer is projected to drain nearly $21 billion from the economy due to lost productivity, cause an additional $102 billion in direct medical costs and create another $140 billion in losses as a result of premature death.[2] While we have made great strides over the past two decades in reducing the rate of death from cancer, we are in danger of falling behind previous generations. Although we have cut in half the percentage of regular tobacco users, 20 percent of the population still smokes,[3] and the rate of childhood obesity due to bad diet and lack of physical activity has reached epic proportions. For the first time in our Nation's history, our children could live shorter lives on average than their parents. I urge you, as our Nation's leaders, not to let that happen.

Every day, nearly 4,000 young people try their first cigarette and approximately 900 become addicted daily smokers. The percentage of children aged 6 to 11 years old in the United States who were obese increased from 7 percent in 1980 to nearly 20 percent in 2008. Similarly, the percentage of adolescents aged 12 to 19 years old who were obese increased from 5 percent to 18 percent over the same period. Obese children and adolescents are likely to be obese as adults and are therefore more at risk for adult health problems such as heart disease, type 2 diabetes, stroke, cancer and osteoarthritis. Furthermore, inadequate access to preventive care and primary health care in minority and low-income populations continues to result in disparities in health outcomes, and the unfortunate result of that will continue to intensify as our country becomes more diverse over time.

As a Nation, we spent more than $2.5 trillion for health care in 2009. We spent far more than other countries in the developed world, yet we delivered a quality of care that ranked below them in life expectancy, infant mortality, and other key indicators. The number of seniors aged 65 and older is projected to increase to 18.5 percent of the total population by 2025, a factor that will help drive health care spending from 16 percent of GDP in 2007 to 25 percent of GDP in 2025, and potentially to 37 percent in 2050.[4] Despite the advances we have made in successfully discovering and treating cancer, the actual number of cancer deaths will increase in the coming years because of the significant growth of the elderly population. In the absence of urgent action, the rising financial and economic costs of chronic disease will reach levels that are beyond our capacity to deal with them.

———

[1] The Global Economic Burden of Non-communicable Diseases. Prepared by the World Economic Forum and the Harvard School of Public Health (2011).

[2] American Cancer Society. Cancer Facts and Figures 2011. Atlanta: American Cancer Society, 2011.

[3] American Cancer Society. Cancer Prevention and Early Detection Facts and Figures 2011. Atlanta: American Cancer Society, 2011.

[4] Congressional Budget Office. The Long Term Budget Outlook (June 2010).

36

PREVENTION IS THE REAL CURE

So what is the answer? How do we as a nation deliver high-quality care to an aging population at a cost we can afford? Certainly, a large part of the answer is through prevention. We know that 50 percent of cancer deaths in America today are preventable. Much of the suffering and death from cancer that occurs today, along with the substantial cost we incur of treating advanced disease, could be reduced through evidence-based prevention. That means more systematic efforts to reduce tobacco use, improve diet and physical activity, reduce obesity, develop and deliver preventive vaccines, and expand the use of established early detection screening tests. Proper utilization of established screening tests and cancer vaccines can prevent the development of certain cancers and premalignant abnormalities. Screening tests can also improve survival and decrease mortality by detecting cancer at an early stage when treatment is more effective.

Throughout history, prevention has been the key to bringing known diseases under control. Prevention in the public health sphere has virtually eliminated epidemics of plague, cholera, yellow fever, measles and polio from our shores. Clean water, mosquito and rodent eradication, and the development of oral and intravenous vaccines—these are all preventive measures. We are able to keep our communities safe through conscious action to prevent diseases from occurring.

This is what we need to do to prevent the next epidemic of cancer, heart disease and diabetes. We must go on the attack now against childhood obesity, tobacco use and other causes of these diseases, or we will be overwhelmed by the cost of treating them later. Today we spend just 3 to 4 percent of our health care dollars on prevention.[5] That's not enough.

INVESTING IN STRATEGIES THAT WORK

A large portion of NCDs are attributable to modifiable risk factors—things we can do something about, such as tobacco use, diet and exercise, and compliance with proven early detection recommendations. So, while we don't expect these diseases to disappear entirely in the near term, here at and around the world we have opportunities to substantially reduce the risk of these diseases and catch them at an earlier more treatable stage simply by encouraging people to act on what we already know and what is proven to work. This would bring down costs for medical care, lost productivity, and other associated costs.

For example, communities with comprehensive tobacco control programs that include cessation services for a wide scope of their population experience faster declines in cigarette sales, smoking prevalence, lung cancer incidence and mortality than States that do not invest in these programs. Tobacco quitlines can increase cessation success by more than 50 percent. In the United States, quitlines reach only about 1 percent of the country's 46 million adult smokers each year.[6] Researchers estimate that with adequate funding and promotional activities, quitlines could reach 16 percent of smokers annually.[7] This could increase the number of tobacco users receiving relatively inexpensive cessation assistance services to 7.1 million smokers per year.[7]

Screening for breast, cervical and colorectal cancers enables doctors to catch these diseases in their early stages, and even to prevent them entirely in the case of colon cancer. Unfortunately, screening rates are far below optimum levels nationwide, resulting in higher costs and worse health outcomes. Colorectal cancer screenings in the United States remain low, with only about half of the population aged 50 and older receiving their recommended tests. Consequently, colorectal cancer takes a significant toll on the Medicare population, both in terms of lives affected and staggering treatment costs. Of the 140,000 people diagnosed with colorectal cancer in 2011, nearly two-thirds were within the Medicare population. In addition, with the introduction of biologics, oncolytics and other targeted therapies, Medicare faces ever increasing costs to treat advanced colorectal cancer with state-of-the-art therapy.

By increasing colorectal cancer screening rates in the population aged 50 to 64, we would reduce suffering, save lives, and reduce cancer costs in Medicare. A recent study by the American Cancer Society found that increasing colorectal screening rates in the pre-Medicare population could reduce subsequent Medicare treatment

[5] Woolf, SH. The Power of Prevention and What It Requires. JAMA. 2008;299(20):2437–2439.
[6] SE Cummins, L Bailey, S Campbell, C Koon-Kirby, SH Zhu. (2007). Tobacco Cessation Quitlines in North America: A Descriptive Study. Tobacco Control;16 (Suppl I):i9–i15.
[7] North American Quitline Consortium. (2009). Tobacco Cessation Quitlines: A Good Investment to Save Lives, Decrease Direct Medical Costs and Increase Productivity. Phoenix, AZ: North American Quitline Consortium.

costs by $15 billion over 11 years.[8] The earlier and sooner regular screening begins, the larger the benefit to Medicare in terms of cancer treatment costs avoided. Investing in screening is a wise use of limited health dollars.

Mammogram screening provided under the National Breast and Cervical Cancer Early Detection Program has detected 52,000 breast cancers over the past 20 years and saved countless lives. Last week I had the honor of attending an event a few blocks away at the Capital Breast Care Center celebrating both National Breast Cancer Awareness Month and the 10 millionth cancer screening administered under the program. These are the kinds of things we are doing now, but we could be doing so much more.

NOW IS THE TIME

We must elevate prevention into standard practice and policy nationwide, and I believe we have begun to do that with passage of health reform legislation in 2010. Some people suggest that patients must have "skin in the game" in the form of out-of-pocket costs to prevent them from overusing health care services. But we know from the evidence that co-pays, deductibles and other out-of-pocket costs actually deter people from seeking preventive care.[9] Patient cost-sharing for preventive services is penny-wise and pound-foolish. This is especially true for those with lower incomes because even a small copay has been shown to discourage getting a simple prevention service.[9]

I have the honor of serving on the national Advisory Group on Prevention, Health Promotion, and Integrative and Public Health, which is charged with providing recommendations on how best to integrate the prevention efforts of the Federal Government and coordinate all prevention and wellness services nationwide. The advisory board helped to develop the first ever National Prevention Strategy to ensure that health and prevention are part of all of our policies and health programs. This comprehensive cross-sector strategy will help us achieve a healthier nation. And I believe the Prevention and Public Health Fund is an important down payment on prevention and wellness. I asked my staff to compile a few examples of how the Prevention and Public Health Fund is helping to reduce cancer risk factors and save lives, and I'll illustrate a few of them here.

In West Virginia, the Department of Health was awarded $1 million in fiscal year 2010 to help improve wellness and prevention efforts. The grant will help combat obesity by evaluating changes in community-level variables (such as changes in cafeteria foods), and the impact on body mass index and related biometric measures. Through this project we will begin to identify effective strategies that can be employed at the community level, which is where it counts.

In another project in Wyoming, $127,000 was allocated over 2 years from the fund to enhance tobacco cessation quitlines. This is a solution to smoking addiction that we know from the evidence works and simply needs to be adequately resourced. I assure you that fewer people in Wyoming will smoke as a result of this investment of tax dollars.

Just last month, the Department of Health and Human Services awarded more than $103 million through its Community Transformation Grants program. Sixty-one private and public organizations in 36 States and one territory will receive funding to promote healthy living and prevention locally over the next 5 years, reaching 120 million Americans. In Washington State, $3.3 million will be used to address five strategic objectives: tobacco-free living; active and healthy eating; high impact evidence-based clinical and other preventive services, specifically prevention and control of high blood pressure; social and emotional wellness; and healthy and safe physical environments. The Maine Department of Health and Human Services received a $1.3 million implementation award to build on existing initiatives like a tobacco helpline and physical activity program for elementary school children, who as we know are otherwise experiencing fewer hours of physical activity in school every year.

CONCLUSION

Today, we know more about cancer than ever before, but while we continue to make important progress, we have not yet realized the true potential we already have to save lives and reduce suffering from this terrible disease. The simple truth

---

[8] National Colorectal Cancer Roundtable. Increasing Colorectal Cancer Screening—Saving Lives and Saving Dollars: Screening 50 to 64 year olds Reduces Cancer Costs to Medicare. September 2007.

[9] Trivedi AN, Rakowski W, Ayanian JZ. Effect of cost sharing on screening mammography in Medicare health plans. N Engl J Med 2008;358:375–83.

is that while more Americans were saved from cancer last year than ever before, it is also true that millions of Americans still suffer and die from cancer. It doesn't have to be this way.

We don't need a magic bullet to control cancer, what we need is the will and courage to do the right things. If we do, we can and will significantly hasten the day when cancer is no longer a significant public health threat in America and around the world.

The CHAIRMAN. Thank you very much, Dr. Seffrin, for that very forceful and poignant testimony.

Mr. Griffin, please proceed.

STATEMENT OF JOHN GRIFFIN, JR., J.D., CHAIRMAN, AMERICAN DIABETES ASSOCIATION, VICTORIA, TX

Mr. GRIFFIN. Thank you, Chairman Harkin, Senator Roberts. It's my privilege, and thank you for allowing me to testify on behalf of the American Diabetes Association and the 105 million Americans with diabetes and pre-diabetes.

Every 17 seconds, a child or an adult is told in this country, "You have diabetes." If current trends continue, we know that one in three children will develop diabetes in their lifetime, and in minority communities where I come from, one in two children will have diabetes in their lifetime.

It is an economic tsunami for our country—diabetes. The complications are severe. Today, 328 Americans will have an amputation. Another 120 will enter end stage kidney problems, dialysis problems. Another 48 will be blind, all because of diabetes. Diabetes also takes a vengeance on our wallets. The monetary cost of diabetes was almost $220 billion a year in 2007.

Consider this: one in five healthcare dollars in this country and one in three Medicare dollars in this country are associated with diabetes. We know these costs will overwhelm our healthcare system if we don't intervene with prevention. We can do it. For too long, we've acted only when full blown diabetes is present, or act for an amputation or kidney dialysis or eye surgeries instead of preventing.

While we applaud the great prevention work being done at HHS and at the Division of Diabetes Translation, the Federal investment at this point is too small. Among the many facets of the Affordable Care Act is its focus on prevention and its creation of the Prevention and Public Health Fund. We know Type 2 diabetes is preventable, and the best evidence of this is those who live free of diabetes because we prevented it.

Taylor David of the Klamath tribe in Oregon knows prevention works. She had pre-diabetes, but, luckily, the Klamath Diabetes Prevention Program helped her lose more than 38 pounds. She no longer has pre-diabetes. She runs 5Ks now, because she was one of 36 clinical demonstration projects for Native Americans based upon a successful clinical trial at NIH. The proof is there.

The clinical trial found that intervention resulted in weight loss, resulted in more exercise, and caused those to delay—a 58 percent delay in diabetes and prevent diabetes in its participants. Seventy-one percent of seniors reduced their risk for diabetes. Follow up studies show that this intervention can be replicated in community environments for less than $300 a participant, and compare that to an amputation or eye surgery.

The reality is that we can save $190 billion over 10 years if we scale these to a national level. This is not complicated math. Congress actually had this success in mind when it authored the National Diabetes Prevention Program. Thanks to Senator Franken and Senator Lugar for being a leader on this. Recently, the Appropriations Committee proposed funding the program through the Prevention and Public Health Fund.

This represents the best comprehensive national effort to invest in prevention and rein in healthcare costs. The NDPP is the prime example of results we've proven we can get. This is exactly how we should be using taxpayers' resources. We asked scientists to develop a program to prevent diabetes and avoid complications, and they did it. And then they road tested it, and it delayed half the cases of diabetes. These are otherwise people who will be in the circle of diabetes who will ultimately get complications and be a drag on our healthcare dollars.

Then we asked healthcare experts: Can we do this in our communities and cut the costs? And you know what? They did it. Y's are doing it. In the face of this tsunami of exploding diabetes, we found something that actually works and keeps people away from diabetes. We cannot cut the Prevention and Public Health Fund. We simply can't afford not to stop diabetes.

It's not only the ADA and others working on this. As you mentioned, United Healthcare is working on this. They figured it out— a private health insurer. They're saving money by doing proven— clinically proven prevention programs. It was the partnership like that with United Health and the Y that Margaret Hutchinson of Mound, MN, managed to stop diabetes in its tracks.

Margaret had an elevated blood glucose. She was in the zone of danger for diabetes. She got a note that said she was in the danger zone. She got into a Y program—allowed her to lose 13 percent of her body weight, and now she is diabetes-free. However, these programs are not everywhere. They're proven to work, but they're not everywhere and they need to be.

We all want, in this room and other places, to make a difference in the health and financial stability of our country. This committee here has demonstrated a focused commitment to chronic disease prevention, because diabetes and complications are bipartisan. Using the Prevention Fund to invest in programs like the NDPP is an important step.

The American Diabetes Association and the other 26 million children with diabetes, like I've had for 15 years, are standing ready to work with you to make our country healthier and more committed to preventing disease and producing more stories like Taylor's and Margaret's. We can together change the trajectory of the human and financial crisis that diabetes is inflicting on our country, if only we will attack it with a thoughtful and concerted effort that relies on approaches we know work. It is to those approaches that we commend you this afternoon.

Thank you for allowing me this time to be able to share this about diabetes.

[The prepared statement of Mr. Griffin follows:]

40

PREPARED STATEMENT OF JOHN GRIFFIN, JR., J.D.

EXECUTIVE SUMMARY

Prevention is our Nation's greatest untold healthcare story. For far too long we have acted once disease is present in the body rather than supporting efforts to prevent chronic disease. But, with the passage of the Patient Protection and Affordable Care Act (PPACA, Public Law 111–148), prevention became front and center to our efforts to fight disease, encourage healthy living, and rein in costs.

Every 17 seconds somebody is diagnosed with diabetes in the United States. Already nearly 26 million Americans have diabetes, and another 79 million Americans have prediabetes and are at increased risk for developing type 2 diabetes. According to the Centers for Disease Control and Prevention (CDC) one in three adults will have diabetes by the year 2050 if present trends continue. This number is even greater for minority populations with nearly one in two minority adults expected to have diabetes in 2050.

In addition to the physical toll, diabetes also attacks our wallets. The total cost of diabetes to the United States was $218 billion in 2007. Approximately one out of every five health care dollars is spent caring for someone with diagnosed diabetes and nearly one-third of Medicare expenses are associated with treating diabetes and its complications. If we do not work to prevent diabetes, this epidemic will bankrupt our healthcare system.

Despite these grim statistics, we know that type 2 diabetes is largely preventable. Sedentary lifestyles and unhealthy diets contribute greatly to the burden of diabetes and being overweight or obese is a leading modifiable risk factor for type 2 diabetes. Other risk factors include physical inactivity, family history of the disease, being a member of a high-risk population, advanced age and impaired glucose tolerance or impaired fasting glucose. With tens of millions of Americans at risk for diabetes it is crucial that we work to prevent new cases of the disease. Indeed, due to rising healthcare costs, we can't afford not to. A 2008 study by Trust for America's Health found that investment of $10 per person per year in proven community prevention programs could save the country more than $15.6 billion per year within 5 years—a return on investment of $5.60 for every dollar spent.

Individuals at risk for diabetes can prevent the disease through a specific evidence-based lifestyle intervention aimed at diabetes prevention. The Diabetes Prevention Program (DPP), a multicenter clinical research trial funded by the National Institutes of Health's National Institute of Diabetes and Digestive and Kidney Diseases (NIDDK), found that modest weight loss through dietary changes and increased physical activity can prevent or delay the onset of diabetes by 58 percent in participants with prediabetes. Further studies of the DPP by the CDC have shown that this groundbreaking intervention can be replicated in community settings for a cost of less than $300 per participant. With this in mind, Congress authorized the National Diabetes Prevention Program as a part of the PPACA. This program allows CDC to expand these evidence-based lifestyle intervention programs across the country and into communities. For this program to truly thrive across the Nation, we need a strong Federal investment to develop the infrastructure necessary to ensure access to this proven approach, to develop more community-based sites, and to provide public education efforts.

The Prevention and Public Health Fund, which the Senate Appropriations Committee has proposed as a funding source for the National Diabetes Prevention Program, is a monumental national investment in prevention and public health programs. It represents the best comprehensive effort to date to prevent disease and improve the quality of life for millions of Americans. Funding efforts to prevent diabetes is essential to reining in our Nation's ballooning healthcare costs. This year there have been numerous efforts to cut or eliminate the Prevention and Public Health Fund, but doing so would only set our country back in its efforts to rein in health care costs and trim budget deficits.

Physical activity and proper nutrition are essential to reduce the risk for diabetes in children and adults. That's why the Association supports legislative efforts like the FIT Kids Act, last year's Healthy, Hunger-Free Kids Act, and PPACA provisions that require menu labeling in chain restaurants.

The HELP Committee has consistently demonstrated a commitment to chronic disease prevention and the Association is grateful for those efforts. We know we all want to make a difference in the health and financial stability of this Nation. Using the Prevention and Public Health Fund to make a dedicated investment in proven chronic disease prevention programs, including the National Diabetes Prevention Program, is the first step. The Association stands ready to work with Congress toward making America a nation committed to preventing disease rather than acting only to treat disease.

———

Chairman Harkin, Ranking Member Enzi and members of the committee, thank you for providing me the opportunity to testify today before the Committee on Health, Education, Labor, and Pensions (HELP) on behalf of the American Diabetes Association (Association) and the nearly 105 million American children and adults living with diabetes and prediabetes, including myself.

The state of chronic disease prevention is an important topic. Prevention is our Nation's greatest untold healthcare story. For far too long we have acted once disease is present in the body, and often only to mitigate an acute episode, rather than believing in and supporting efforts to prevent chronic disease. But, last year, with the passage of the Patient Protection and Affordable Care Act (PPACA, Public Law 111–148), prevention became front and center to our efforts to fight disease, encourage healthy living, and rein in costs. The inclusion of preventive services as a required benefit, the development of the National Prevention Strategy, and the establishment of the Prevention and Public Health Fund, are major steps to put our country on the right track to prevent chronic diseases like diabetes. In my testimony, I will present the facts about prevention, but I will also tell the stories behind it that prove prevention works and we all have a role to play in promoting it.

Every 17 seconds somebody is diagnosed with diabetes in the United States. Already nearly 26 million Americans have diabetes, but this number is expected to grow to 44 million in the next 25 years if current trends continue. Another 79 million Americans have prediabetes and are at increased risk for developing type 2 diabetes. For these millions of Americans, the complications of diabetes are severe. Two out of three people with diabetes die from heart disease or stroke. Today 238 Americans will undergo an amputation; 120 will enter end-stage kidney disease programs; and 48 will become blind—all due to the devastating effects of this disease. In fact, diabetes is the leading cause of kidney failure, adult-onset blindness and non-traumatic lower-limb amputation, as well as a major cause of cardiovascular disease and stroke.

According to the Centers for Disease Control and Prevention (CDC) one in three adults will have diabetes by the year 2050 if we do not take action. This number is even greater for minority populations with nearly one in two minority adults expected to have diabetes in 2050.

In addition to the physical toll, diabetes also attacks our wallets. A study by the Lewin Group found that in 2007 the total cost to our country of diabetes and its complications, along with gestational diabetes, undiagnosed diabetes and prediabetes, was $218 billion. Medical expenditures due to diabetes totaled $116 billion, including $27 billion for diabetes care, $58 billion for chronic diabetes-related complications, and $31 billion for excess general medical costs. Other costs included $18 billion for undiagnosed diabetes, $25 billion for prediabetes and $623 million for gestational diabetes. Indirect costs resulting from increased absenteeism, reduced productivity, disease-related unemployment disability and loss of productive capacity due to early mortality reached $58 billion. Approximately one out of every five health care dollars is spent caring for someone with diagnosed diabetes. Further, one-third of Medicare expenses are associated with treating diabetes and its complications. Clearly, if we do not work to prevent diabetes this epidemic will bankrupt our healthcare system.

Diabetes is a chronic disease that impairs the body's ability to use food for energy. The hormone insulin, which is made in the pancreas, is needed for the body to change food into energy. In people with diabetes, either the pancreas does not create insulin, which is type 1 diabetes, or the body does not create enough insulin and/ or cells are resistant to insulin, which is type 2 diabetes. In individuals with prediabetes, blood glucose levels are higher than normal and the risk for developing type 2 diabetes is elevated. If left untreated, diabetes results in too much glucose in the blood stream. The majority of diabetes cases, 90 to 95 percent, are type 2 diabetes. Additionally, an estimated 18 percent of pregnancies are affected by gestational diabetes, which occurs when a mother's blood glucose levels are too high during pregnancy, which can harm both the mother and her baby. In the short term, blood glucose levels that are too high or too low (as a result of medication to treat diabetes) can be life threatening. The long-term complications of diabetes are widespread, serious—and deadly.

Despite these grim statistics, we know that type 2 diabetes is largely preventable. Being overweight or obese is a leading modifiable risk factor for type 2 diabetes. In addition to obesity, there are several known risk factors for type 2 diabetes, including physical inactivity, unhealthy diets, family history of the disease, being a member of a high-risk population, advanced age and previous impaired glucose tolerance or impaired fasting glucose. Although some of these factors are not subject to change, changing one's lifestyle can often help prevent type 2 diabetes.

With tens of millions of Americans at risk for diabetes it is crucial that we work to prevent new cases of the disease. Indeed, given rising healthcare costs, we can't afford not to. A 2008 study by Trust for America's Health found that investment of $10 per person per year in proven community prevention programs could save the country more than $15.6 billion per year within 5 years—a return on investment of $5.60 for every dollar spent. Investing in prevention programs will save money and improve the health and quality of life of Americans, two outcomes that, as a Nation, we cannot afford to ignore.

NATIONAL DIABETES PREVENTION PROGRAM

Research has shown that over half of the individuals at risk for diabetes can prevent the disease through a specific evidence-based lifestyle intervention aimed at diabetes prevention. The National Diabetes Prevention Program, included in the Patient Protection and Affordable Care Act (PPACA), authorizes CDC to expand its work in translating a successful National Institutes of Health (NIH) clinical trial to the community setting for individuals with the highest risk of developing diabetes.

The Diabetes Prevention Program (DPP), a multicenter clinical research trial funded by the NIH's National Institute of Diabetes and Digestive and Kidney Diseases (NIDDK), found that a structured lifestyle intervention given in a clinical setting that produced a modest weight loss (about 5–7 percent of body weight) through dietary changes and increased physical activity was able to prevent or delay the onset of diabetes by 58 percent in participants with prediabetes—those at the highest risk for diabetes. The results were even greater among adults aged 60 years or older, who reduced their risk by 71 percent. Further studies of the DPP by the CDC have shown that this groundbreaking intervention can be replicated in community settings for a cost of less than $300 per participant, about a fourth of the cost of the original clinical intervention. With this in mind, Congress authorized the CDC to operate the National Diabetes Prevention Program. This program allows CDC to build the infrastructure to expand these evidence-based lifestyle intervention programs to reach communities across the country. Bringing this program to scale is the key to prevention for many of the 79 million Americans with prediabetes.

Researchers have continued to follow clinical trial participants. Ten years later, the Diabetes Prevention Program Outcomes Study found that the rate of developing diabetes was still reduced. Moreover, individuals aged 60 years or older still showed the greatest overall reduction, proving that the results of this program continue in the long term.

The National Diabetes Prevention Program supports the creation of community-based sites where trained staff will provide those at high risk for diabetes with cost-effective, group-based lifestyle intervention programs. Local sites will be required to provide an approved curriculum and trained instructors and will be rigorously evaluated based on program standards and goals. Thus, implementation of the National Diabetes Prevention Program will ensure availability of a low-cost, highly successful diabetes prevention program in communities across the country.

The National Diabetes Prevention Program will do more than just prevent diabetes and its devastating complications. Contrary to arguments that prevention does not save money, the National Diabetes Prevention Program shows that prevention programs are a wise investment that yields significant savings. In 2009, the Urban Institute estimated that a nationwide expansion of this type of diabetes prevention program will produce an estimated $190 billion in savings to the U.S. healthcare system over 10 years. Because the burden of chronic disease falls disproportionately on seniors and the poor, the Urban Institute also estimated that 75 percent of the total savings would be to Federal health programs like Medicare and Medicaid. Without a concerted effort at prevention that cost will only grow. Because the National Diabetes Prevention Program focuses on individuals at the highest risk for the disease, the return on investment is certain and it is realized early.

One need only look to the numerous stories of how prevention has changed lives to know that prevention works. Taylor David of the Klamath tribe in Oregon knows that prevention—the Diabetes Prevention Program in particular—works. Taylor was diagnosed with prediabetes. But luckily for her, the Klamath Diabetes Prevention Program was one of the 36 federally funded demonstration projects to translate the DPP clinical trial to meet the cultural needs of tribal organizations.

In 2004, Congress mandated the Indian Health Service (IHS) use additional funding provided through the Special Diabetes Program for Indians (SDPI) to implement the latest scientific findings to prevent diabetes. This resulted in 36 IHS tribal and urban Indian health programs receiving funding to translate the DPP into common prevention education programs in Native American communities. Taylor successfully participated in the program and changed the course of her path to diabetes. She lost over 38 pounds and she no longer has prediabetes. In fact, last year she participated in her first 5k ever and learned how to snowboard. She is healthier, more active, and diabetes free and she states she would not have had the courage, knowledge or ability to make these crucial lifestyle changes were it not for the Klamath Diabetes Prevention Program.

While the National Diabetes Prevention Program has been authorized, it has yet to receive dedicated Federal funding. On September 21, 2011, the Senate Appropriations Committee passed their fiscal year (FY) 2012 Labor, Health and Human Services, and Education Appropriations bill, providing $10 million in funding to the National Diabetes Prevention Program through the Prevention and Public Health Fund. The Association thanks the committee and hopes that Congress and the Administration maintain this funding as the fiscal year 2010 appropriations process continues. Despite the lack of Federal funding needed to fully scale this program, CDC, the Y-USA and UnitedHealth Group have partnered with great success to administer this program in 170 sites in 23 States. This is a start, but it leaves most of the 79 million Americans at risk for diabetes without access to this program, and doctors with nowhere to refer patients with prediabetes. For this program to truly thrive across the Nation, it needs a strong Federal investment to develop the infrastructure necessary to ensure access to this proven approach, to develop more community-based sites, and to provide public education.

This year the Administration released the National Prevention Strategy, which promises the Federal Government will "promote and expand research efforts to identify high-priority clinical and community preventive services and test innovative strategies to support delivery of these services." This is a laudable goal, but in the case of the National Diabetes Prevention Program, the research has been done, the results already exist and the Federal Government is poised to take the next step. That next step is a commitment to bringing the results of this successful, federally funded research to communities across our country.

Funding will lead to more stories like Margaret Hutchinson from Mound, MN. Last year at Margaret's annual check-up, she found out her blood glucose levels were elevated. Not having a family history of diabetes she didn't think much about it, until she received a letter—and a wake-up call—from her insurer telling her that she had prediabetes and was eligible for the Diabetes Prevention Program at her local Y.

Margaret started the program in November of last year, attended weekly classes with a small group and a lifestyle coach who taught the participants about proper nutrition and physical activity. The class tracked their diets, activities and weight on a weekly basis to decrease their risk for diabetes. Margaret far surpassed the goal to lose 7 percent of her body weight, dropping 13 percent plus an additional 10 pounds after the weekly classes ended. Her blood glucose levels no longer indicate prediabetes. She is now much less likely to develop type 2 diabetes and to seek treatment for its dangerous and costly complications.

Indeed, this program is *exactly* how we should be using taxpayer funds. We asked our scientists to develop a program to prevent diabetes. They did so and they tested it in the doctor's office. It prevented or delayed over half of the new cases of diabetes. Then we asked our public health experts to see if we could move this great program into the community and slash the price. They did it. In the face of the tsunami that is diabetes, we found something that works! To discontinue the Federal investment in prevention by eliminating the Prevention and Public Health Fund would be a slap in the face of the success we have achieved as a nation.

PREVENTION AND PUBLIC HEALTH FUND

The Prevention and Public Health Fund, which the Senate Appropriations Committee has proposed as a funding source for the National Diabetes Prevention Program, is a monumental national investment in prevention and public health programs. We applaud the great work being done regarding prevention at HHS and specifically at the Division of Diabetes Translation, but recognize that the Federal investment just hasn't been adequate. The Prevention and Public Health Fund represents the best comprehensive effort to date to prevent disease and improve the quality of life for millions of Americans. Additionally, funding efforts to prevent chronic diseases, like diabetes and its complications, is essential to reining in our Nation's ballooning healthcare costs.

In this time of tight budgets and drastic proposed funding cuts it is important that Congress protect the Prevention and Public Health Fund. The $218 billion annual price tag of diabetes alone is enough to demonstrate that a concerted effort at chronic disease prevention is a prudent investment. This year, there have been numerous efforts to cut or eliminate the Prevention and Public Health Fund, but doing so would only set our country back in its efforts to rein in health care costs and trim budget deficits. Billions of dollars a year are spent through Federal Government programs to treat acute illnesses and chronic health problems. However, until the creation of the Prevention and Public Health Fund, there was no parallel investment in wellness and chronic disease prevention that could alleviate the existing burden to Federal health programs. Even the CDC's efforts to prevent disease have been hampered by budget cuts and flat funding despite the excellent work they do toward disease prevention. But, with the Prevention and Public Health Fund we are finally seeing that investment. States and communities are using these funds for tobacco cessation, behavioral health, obesity prevention and to strengthen the public health workforce

PHYSICAL ACTIVITY

We know that with healthy diets and active lifestyles, people can reduce their risk for type 2 diabetes. The Physical Activity Guidelines for Americans recommend that adults get 2½ hours of moderate exercise every week to achieve health benefits and reduce the risk of type 2 diabetes, heart disease, stroke and high blood pressure. The guidelines also recommend children be active for at least 1 hour per day to achieve similar health benefits. Our education system must take our children's physical education as seriously as training their minds if we hope to change the prediction that one in three children (and one in two minority children) born in the year 2000 face a future with diabetes.

This is why the Association supports S. 576, the Fitness Integrated in Teaching (FIT) Kids Act of 2011 sponsored by Chairman Harkin. The FIT Kids Act requires State and local education agencies to include information on health and physical education programs on their annual agency report cards. Requiring this reporting will make school programs more transparent and encourage improved physical education curriculums. This legislation also promotes professional development and training for physical education teachers and emphasizes the importance of promoting healthy lifestyles for students. We ask that the HELP Committee include this legislation in the upcoming reauthorization of the Elementary and Secondary Education Act.

Physical activity can help adults at high risk for the disease prevent type 2 diabetes. Christie Lussoro of the Nez Perce tribe in Idaho has a history of diabetes on both sides of her family. She was concerned about developing diabetes so she joined the Nimiipuu Health Diabetes Program to begin an exercise program and reduce her risk. She worked closely with program staff to develop a customized plan and increased her physical activity level. Over time, Christy lost 31 pounds and her children have joined her at the fitness center to help reduce their own chances of developing type 2 diabetes.

NUTRITION

Access to a healthy diet is essential for all Americans and perhaps can be seen most acutely in children like Ahni. Since moving to the United States from China about 10 years ago, Ahni has adopted a western diet—full of fast foods, processed foods and high-calorie snacks. Even at school, Ahni eats meals that are high in fat, sugars and calories. Moreover, Ahni's school is one of the many that has cut physical education programs. Unfortunately, unless Ahni's family makes drastic changes in their lifestyle and diet, Ahni has a high probability of developing diabetes. Asian Americans are already acutely susceptible to type 2 diabetes, developing the disease at lower weights than people of other races, so Ahni's sedentary lifestyle and high-calorie diet put her even more at risk.

Ahni should be eating healthier meals, especially in school where she spends much of her time. In the 111th Congress, the Association supported passage of the S. 3307, the Healthy, Hunger-Free Kids Act of 2010 (Public Law 111–296). This legislation is a tremendous step forward in improving the nutritional value of foods served at schools. The U.S. Department of Agriculture is moving forward with regulations that will make meals under the Federal school lunch and school breakfast programs healthier and we will soon see improved nutrition standards for foods sold in vending machines, a la carte lines, and school stores as well. In order to curb obesity and the related chronic diseases, like diabetes, it is essential to provide young students with healthy meals and snacks that are low in calories and fat. We ask that Congress oppose any efforts to roll back provisions of this law and allow the relevant Federal agencies to proceed with implementation so our young students can benefit from healthier meals as soon as possible.

The Association also looks forward to final regulations from the Food and Drug Administration implementing the PPACA requirement for chain restaurants to include calorie counts on their menus and menu boards. This information will help people make more informed choices about the food they choose in restaurants. Choosing lower calorie options when dining in restaurants and fast food establishments will help consumers manage their weight and reduce their risk of type 2 diabetes or better manage existing diabetes.

AMERICAN DIABETES ASSOCIATION ACTIVITIES

The Federal Government is not in this alone. The American Diabetes Association is also doing its part to promote prevention and improve lives. We are engaging in continuing education for clinicians, ensuring that providers are familiar with the preventive tools that are available to them so that they can provide the best options for at-risk patients. For individuals, the Association provides information about diabetes and its seriousness, education on how to lower their risk for diabetes as well as inspiration and programs in communities across the country. Between PSA campaigns to make sure people know their risk for diabetes and education on how to lower that risk, we are getting the message out that it is crucial to stop diabetes.

Additionally, along with the American Cancer Society and the American Heart Association, we have established the Preventive Health Partnership (PHP). The PHP is a coordinated effort between our three organizations to raise public awareness about what Americans need to do to live healthier lives and to provide information and motivation about how better nutrition and regular exercise can prevent type 2 diabetes, heart disease and some forms of cancer.

CONCLUSION

We all want to make a difference in the health and financial stability of this Nation. The HELP Committee has consistently demonstrated a commitment to chronic disease prevention and the Association is grateful for those efforts. Your leadership in combating the growing epidemic of diabetes is critical. It is clear that in order to stop diabetes and rein in healthcare costs, we must support efforts to prevent chronic disease and the complications associated with chronic disease.

Using the Prevention and Public Health Fund to make a dedicated investment in proven chronic disease prevention programs, including the National Diabetes Prevention Program, is the first step. As we sit here today, there are patients in our Nation's hospitals awaiting a horrific amputation or waiting in line at the clinic for their turn at kidney dialysis. Let's work together to clear those waiting rooms and, instead, have more stories like Taylor and Margaret. The Association stands ready to work with Congress toward making America a nation committed to preventing disease rather than acting only to treat disease. Thank you again for allowing me to testify before the committee today.

The CHAIRMAN. Mr. Griffin, thanks for a very clear and very forceful presentation. We appreciate that.

Dr. Troy, please proceed.

STATEMENT OF TEVI TROY, Ph.D., SENIOR FELLOW, HUDSON INSTITUTE, WASHINGTON, DC

Mr. TROY. Mr. Chairman, thank you very much for this opportunity.

And thank you as well to Senator Roberts and Senator Franken, before whom I've had the privilege to testify in the past.

I think we can all agree after today's conversation that obesity is a problem, chronic diseases are a problem. I like to talk about it from three specific perspectives. One is from a health concern, and we've talked about it already a great deal today. But two-thirds of Americans are overweight or obese. Over 60 million people have diabetes. And Type 2 diabetes, as we've discussed, is both preventable but also a terrible condition.

From an economic perspective, and specifically from an employment perspective, I cite in my testimony, which I appreciate you putting in the record, that obesity has employment costs equivalent to about 1.8 million workers per year at $42,000 each. But when we think about it in times of consistently high unemployment rates—and the rate was just 9.1 percent last week—we should really think about the employment costs of obesity and chronic diseases.

And then I'm also very worried from a national security perspective. The Army did a study that found that 27 percent of Americans, age 17 to 24, are too overweight to serve. And the Pentagon spends about a billion dollars a year trying to deal with obesity in members of the armed forces.

So recognizing that this is a problem, the question is how to approach it. And I commend the committee today for asking a lot of the right questions, because while I agree that prevention works, that doesn't mean that all prevention programs work. In fact, I cite in my testimony some CBO statements that suggest that sometimes prevention programs lead to higher utilization and higher medical spending. So we have to be very careful about it.

So, therefore, I lay out a number of ways to do this in the right way, in the ways that will actually use the Federal dollars in the best way and make sure that we are addressing the problem. So I think to the extent we have Federal programs for this and that dollars need to be discretionary, they need to be done in a budget conscious way, recognizing our $1.4 trillion deficit and our $14 trillion debt.

I also think it needs to be targeted, accountable—and I appreciate all the questions today about accountability and the need for metrics to make sure that to the extent we do have programs, that they are measured and that they are working. And they also should be done in a competitive and a political process. And also, Senator Roberts mentioned that they need to be done in a cooperative process. It doesn't really help a county if they get a grant and they are not prepared for the grant and don't know what to do with the grant.

I also think that from the perspective of public health advocates who recognize the importance of prevention, you need to think about the optics of it as well. If prevention dollars are wasted or ineffective, that can set back the cause of prevention funding for everybody who's concerned about this area.

I also think it's important that we look at private sector solutions. And I'm glad that some of those private sector solutions, such as employee wellness programs, were mentioned. I believe Senator Franken said there was a four-to-one benefit ratio. I cite some programs that have a three-to-one benefit ratio. Four-to-one is better than three-to-one, but both are good.

I think it's important that we get an incentive-based approach to this, to get individuals involved in their own health and that they have their own incentives to get fit and to engage in prevention activities on their own. I suggest some other possibilities, private sector possibilities, such as health savings accounts, which help build a consumer-driven health system, and also differential premiums—which I know the Senate has done some work on this here, which I appreciate. So I think all those are helpful.

I also think to the extent that we encourage the private sector to engage in this, we need to be careful not to micromanage private sector activity and make sure that it can develop organically and in the most efficient and effective way.

So in sum, I think preventative medicine can prove to be a prudent investment. But in order to be effective, as I said, it must take place within the limits of our significant fiscal challenges and must be done in such a way that the services eligible are not too broadly defined and narrowly targeted. And it must take place within the context of a strong commitment to rigorous program evaluation.

Mr. Chairman and other members of the committee, thank you for your time and for your devotion to this issue.

[The prepared statement of Dr. Troy follows:]

PREPARED STATEMENT OF TEVI TROY, PH.D.

Mr. Chairman, Mr. Ranking Member, members of the committee, chronic diseases cost this country more than $750 billion annually, and present a serious challenge to the United States from a health, economic, and national security perspective:

• Health concerns: Two thirds of Americans are overweight or obese; over 16 million people have diabetes, and type 2 diabetes is a preventable condition.

• Economic concerns: Obesity has employment costs equivalent to about 1.8 million workers per year at $42,000 each.

• National Security concerns: The Army found 27 percent of Americans aged 17 to 24 too overweight to serve. The Pentagon spends $1 billion a year dealing with obesity.

Ad campaigns, such as those done by the Bush and Obama administrations, are nice, but not working. We need a more serious strategy, so it makes sense to be talking about prevention of the problem.

Prevention is important, but must be done the right way. Prevention dollars should be discretionary, targeted, accountable, and go through a competitive and apolitical process. In addition, we must remember that prevention does not always lead to cost savings. In addition, labeling a project "prevention" does not mean it will be cost-effective. Wasteful or ineffective prevention spending is not helpful from a messaging standpoint, and is particularly problematic at a time when we have an enormous budget deficit and face a $14 trillion—and growing—debt.

We also need to look at private sector solutions: employee fitness programs, Health Savings Accounts, differential premiums, and other forms of incentive-based approaches. To be successful in our prevention efforts, we need to unleash the power of incentives and move toward a more consumer-driven system, one that will encourage individuals to make healthy choices for themselves and their families. At the same time, we should encourage the private sector in this effort without micromanaging.

In sum, preventive medicine can prove to be a prudent investment in the future of our country, but in order to be effective it must: take place within the limits of our significant fiscal challenges; be done in such a way that the services eligible are not too broadly defined; and take place within the context of a strong commitment to rigorous program evaluation.

Mr. Chairman, Mr. Ranking Member, members of the committee, I thank you for your time and your efforts to fight chronic disease.

––––––

Mr. Chairman, Mr. Ranking Member, members of the committee, my name is Tevi Troy, and I am a senior fellow at Hudson Institute, and a former Deputy Secretary of the U.S. Department of Health and Human Services, as well as a former senior White House Domestic Policy Aide. In both capacities, I was involved in the Bush administration's efforts to combat obesity and promote preventive behaviors.

I come here before the committee to talk about the important issue of prevention, particularly prevention of chronic diseases, treatment of which costs this country more than $750 billion annually.

I support the use of funds for appropriate preventive healthcare measures. As Benjamin Franklin wisely put it, "An ounce of prevention is worth a pound of cure."

I also recognize that there is a lot to prevent. The current State of healthcare in America is well past due for its "ounce of prevention." I recognize that the concept

48

of "prevention" addresses multiple concerns, including smoking, but I will focus here on the rising obesity epidemic as an illustrative example. Currently, two-thirds of Americans are overweight or obese. This number is increasing at an annual rate of 1.1 percent, or by about 2.4 million new obese adults each year. As you well know, obesity increases the likelihood for several other co-morbidities, including hypertension, type II diabetes, coronary heart disease, and stroke, each with its own range of associated costs and health complications. With respect to diabetes alone, CDC has found over 16 million people have this terrible, and often preventable, condition.

From an economic perspective, estimates of the cost of obesity to America range from $150–$250 billion annually. $3.9 billion alone stemmed from lost productivity due to obesity, reflecting 39.2 million lost days of work. In addition to increased absenteeism, another study, in the *Journal of Environmental and Occupational Medicine,* found presenteeism—decreased productivity of employees while at work—to be a significant cost-driver as well. Specifically, the cost of obesity among full-time employees was estimated to be $73.1 billion—"roughly equivalent to the cost of hiring an additional 1.8 million workers per year at $42,000 each, which is roughly the average annual wages of U.S. workers." At a time of consistently high unemployment, which was 9.1 percent in the most recent report, we need to look at the costs of obesity and those costs' potential impact on U.S. employment levels.

Obesity is no longer solely an economic or a health issue, although it is a serious concern in those areas. Obesity has become an issue of national defense as well; the Army found 27 percent of Americans in prime years for military recruitment—17 to 24—were "too overweight to serve in the military." The Pentagon alone spends nearly $1 billion each year coping with weight-related challenges. Retired Rear Adm. James A. Barnett put the issue starkly, warning that "[o]ur national security in the year 2030 is absolutely dependent on reversing the alarming rates of child obesity.

And yet, we must remember that Dr. Franklin's maxim was aimed at promoting cost-effectiveness, which is a value we must keep in mind throughout this conversation. While I am passionate about the need to address obesity and other issues that lead to preventable health conditions, I am not convinced that the government has all of the answers to this problem. In the administration for which I worked, HHS, then led by Secretary Mike Leavitt, worked with the Ad Council and Dreamworks on a public service announcement with characters from the movie Shrek encouraging kids to "Be a Player. Get up and play an hour a day." The Obama administration has followed suit in this regard, making combating obesity one of First Lady Michele Obama's signature initiatives. In February 2010, she launched "Let's Move!," a campaign designed to end obesity in a generation. While the Bush White House did its PR partnership with *Shrek,* Obama opted for New York Yankee star Curtis Granderson, who said kids should play fewer video games and engage in more outdoor activities. Neither admittedly well-intentioned effort is going to stem the obesity tide. So going forward, we need not just good intentions, but also strong principles to guide us, such as the need for the right process, a recognition of our dire fiscal situation, a need for focused and not vaguely defined programs, and a recognition that many so-called prevention savings never materialize.

From a process standpoint, prevention dollars should be discretionary and go through the normal and rigorous appropriations process. As you all well know, spending on the mandatory side of the budget is harder to adjust than discretionary spending because it does not have to compete against other priorities in the annual appropriations process. This means that cost-savings must come disproportionately from the discretionary side of the budget. At a time when both Social Security and Medicare are facing severe funding challenges, when we have a $1.4 trillion deficit and $14 trillion debt, putting more dollars in mandatory accounts lessens the sacrosanct status of mandatory spending writ large, and also will put more pressure on our discretionary accounts to find needed cost savings. The irony here is that increased mandatory spending could increase the pressure to cut discretionary spending on prevention, even if such spending has been shown to be effective.

Another important principle is focus. Programs or studies eligible for funding should not be too broadly defined. Laxity of definition may lead to spending in areas that are not directly related to prevention. Already there has been criticism around one program authorizing Federal funding for the construction of sidewalks and jungle gyms. Programs should be targeted so as not to incur such criticism, which can damage the prevention "brand." Furthermore, since money is fungible, governments facing severe fiscal constraints could potentially use poorly targeted money for ancillary purposes.

In addition, I recognize the importance of rigor in the review process to get the best results. In order to have maximum effectiveness, dollars should be distributed via a competitive process. Policymakers should keep in mind the risk posed by the spending of Federal dollars with inadequate supervision or the ability to correct abuses. A single flawed project can be subject to ridicule—as we have seen with the Solyndra project—and therefore harm the entire endeavor by creating the perception that the program misuses taxpayer dollars. Prevention funding must be targeted so that we are dedicating enough resources to make an impact that actually reduces childhood obesity in the long run. We currently fund over 300 different obesity programs, which suggests an insufficiently focused approach and increases the risk of duplicative or ineffective spending. We must ensure that prevention dollars are spent wisely, and not used to fund parochial projects that do not advance the prevention goal.

In addition, it is important to remember that the "prevention" label itself does not necessarily lead to cost savings. As Robert Gould, president of Partnership for Prevention, has said, "Some preventive services save money and some don't." Just labeling something a "preventive" service does not mean that it prevents anything, or that it will save money. A recent letter by Congressional Budget Office Director Douglas Elmendorf underscores this point. According to Elmendorf, "the evidence suggests that for most preventive services, expanded utilization leads to higher, not lower, medical spending overall." This is because, as Elmendorf noted, doctors, whatever their skill level, are not prophets: "[I]t is important to recognize that doctors do not know beforehand which patients are going to develop costly illnesses." As a result, insufficiently targeted "preventive services" end up adding to total costs because they are too often used on those who will not develop expensive conditions. We need personalized medicine to play a role here. If we can target those with the greatest risk, we will be more likely to have cost-effective interventions.

Even beyond CBO, a recent study by Rutgers University Professor Louise Russell found "that contrary to common belief, prevention usually increases medical spending." The same study found that "Less than 20 percent of the preventive options (and a similar percentage for treatment) fall in the cost-saving category—80 percent add more to medical costs than they save."

Dr. Russell, does, however, open her study with some positive words on preventive spending: "Careful choices about frequency, groups to target, and component costs can increase the likelihood that interventions will be highly cost-effective or even cost-saving." I fully agree. We must find an alternative approach to this very real problem. With this in mind, I would like to highlight one type of program that has proven to be both effective and cost efficient: employee fitness programs. Both Motorola and PepsiCo received at least a $3:1 return on investment from their employee fitness programs. These are private sector initiatives that do not cost the government money, but do help reduce obesity and other preventable conditions. We should encourage these initiatives and let them develop without micromanagement, as maintaining autonomy in employer-sponsored wellness programs is imperative. Government intervention in the design and administration of these programs will likely discourage employers from engaging in this worthy endeavor. In addition, consumer-driven health care, promoted by programs such as Health Savings Accounts, will give individuals additional financial incentives to take the steps necessary to pursue prevention on their own initiative. I would also like to see the Senate continue to work to give the private sector flexibility to promote prevention in the workplace, including the use of differential premium costs to encourage healthy behavior.

I believe a new focus on preventive medicine can prove to be a prudent investment in the future of our country. While doing so, we must not forget the severe fiscal challenges that other important government programs such as Medicare or Social Security already face. We must ensure that the services eligible are not too broadly defined, and that we maintain a strong commitment to rigorous program evaluation. Most importantly, we must proceed in a cost-effective manner, targeting those areas that are both the safest and most cost-effective. And we should unleash the power of incentives and try to move toward a more consumer-driven system, one that will encourage individuals to make healthy choices for themselves and their families. As I have tried to show in my testimony, there is so much at stake in getting this right.

Mr. Chairman, Mr. Ranking Member, members of the committee, I thank you for your time here today, and for your efforts on behalf of prevention.

The CHAIRMAN. Thank you very much, Dr. Troy, again for your very forceful presentation. Appreciate it very, very much.

We'll begin a round of 5-minute questions here.

Ms. Brown, you talked about some—you all had statistics that are frightening. You pointed out, Ms. Brown, that the number of preschoolers who are overweight jumped 36 percent just in the last 10 years, and that is just frightening. And so we have to get at these things early in life, early in life.

But one of the things that—you asked a question in your testimony. You said that all of the findings that we have and lessons learned beg the questions: Why is prevention taking a back seat to acute care and treatment? Why aren't more efforts and dollars being spent on prevention? You say, well, the answers aren't easy. You say prevention first is a long-term commitment policy, long-term. And most of us around here are interested in short-term fixes.

But that's true of human nature. People want to be able to live their lives however they want to live, and I want that pill. I want that magic pill that will make it all right—clean me all up again and start me over again, and all that kind of stuff. So it's kind of human nature.

That's why we look for systems approaches, and that's why I keep emphasizing that we need it early on, and it's got to be broad-based—early on, childhood, preschool settings, neighborhoods, communities, schools, certainly in the homes, but also in the workplace. And that's one place where I have found in the past some private sector employers have been way ahead of the curve on this.

I have examples that go back 25 years of employers in my State that decided to put in wellness programs in their plants, prevention, cut down on smoking. They gave incentives to workers, benefits—some of them pretty nice benefits—if they would see an in-house nutritionist, dietician, something like that, and cut down on smoking. And what we found was that in these early days, their productivity shot up.

See, you always look at the cost, but their productivity went up, turnover rates went down, absenteeism went down. Workers would stay overtime just to make sure everything was right. Nobody was rushing to the door. We know these things work. But why aren't more employers doing it?

We know they work. We know they're cost-effective. As I said, there are some employers that have really done great jobs in this. But how can we—let's face it. We spend most of our days at work. How can we get more employers involved in wellness and prevention?

Ms. BROWN. Well, thank you for that question. Certainly, one of the priorities of the American Heart Association and our partners, the American Cancer Society and the American Diabetes Association, is to get more workplaces to promote the workplace as a location for promoting positive health. We recognize, as you've said, Senator, that people spend a good majority of their day in the workplace.

And if we can encourage employers to offer positive reinforcement for a healthier workplace—so serving healthier foods in the workplace, offering time for individuals in the workplace to get physical activity, helping to promote tobacco cessation programs, and other activities—all very important. So we need to have an environment where employers are provided incentives for doing that in their workplace. And that certainly is a priority for the AHA.

The CHAIRMAN. Dr. Seffrin, what do we need to get more employers—do we need tax benefits? Do we need credit? What do we need to do?

Mr. SEFFRIN. I think the answer, in addition to what Nancy has said, is get specific engagement. We have a program in the American Cancer Society called CEOs Against Cancer. We just had a meeting 3 weeks ago in New York chaired by Glenn Tilton, the former CEO of United Airlines, now the Chairman of JP Morgan Chase.

When they recruit their colleague CEOs and get together and talk, it bypasses a level of strata in the corporation and they can begin to talk about we do care about our employees, and we know a healthier workforce is a more productive workforce. The data are very clear on that.

We've done analyses showing that if a company develops what we call the CEO gold standard on cancer and they provide to their employees the kinds of tests—if they need age appropriate tests—that if they have a stable workforce over 5 years, it becomes budget neutral and then saves them money. So I think it's engagement at the top level. But I see more and more companies being willing to sit down and talk and do something about it.

The CHAIRMAN. Mr. Griffin.

Mr. GRIFFIN. We also at the ADA have relationships with CEOs in large businesses. But part of this is awareness. And we talked about United Health. It's just one carrier, but the message is there. I also want to stress with my friends that up here on the stage we have what we call the Preventive Health Partnership. We found that these organizations together—more than 100 million Americans in our constituency—when Heart, Cancer, and Diabetes stands for these sorts of wellness and the costs that they will save in the long run in terms of prevention that we're learning, we pack a pretty good punch when these three organizations join together, which we are doing now.

The CHAIRMAN. Dr. Troy.

Mr. TROY. Yes, thank you. Two things, one on a positive side— I think that government officials and senior officials can help encourage this. Mrs. Obama, the First Lady, talks about wellness so that she can help encourage CEOs. Similarly, President Bush did programs like that.

But I also think you want to keep employers in the game. Former CBO director, Douglas Holtz-Eakin, has suggested that the Affordable Care Act will lead to a lot of employer dumping, in which employers will no longer have responsibility for the healthcare of their employees. They will put them into the exchanges. To the extent that happens, you'll have employers less interested rather than more interested, and I'm worried about that.

The CHAIRMAN. Very interesting. I've got to look at that. Thank you very much. My time is well over.

Senator Roberts.

Senator ROBERTS. Dr. Seffrin, how many of those CEOs that you met with on prevention have taken the PSA test for prostate cancer? Most of them?

Mr. SEFFRIN. I suspect so.

Senator ROBERTS. Well, the USPSTF has just come out with a recommendation to downgrade PSA screening, if not to get rid of it, for early detection of prostate cancer, recommending that men should no longer need or get the PSA test. It goes by age, and most of the Senate would be interested.

At any rate, you talk prevention, prevention, prevention. Would you like to comment on what the recommendation of the USPSTF is—I know it isn't in final form yet, but it's been leaked out. Any comments?

Mr. SEFFRIN. I'd make a couple of comments. One is that the derating clearly discourages its use, and they're basing that on reviewing a number of studies and two—including two randomized controlled trials which failed to demonstrate a benefit and, indeed, indicate some risks associated—serious risks associated with it.

So when you talk evidence-based—and you mentioned it earlier, Senator Roberts, and, certainly, you did, Senator Harkin—you have to—if that's going to be the standard, you have to pay attention to it. The data are the data.

The American Cancer Society says things a little differently. We feel that there is a test, and, unfortunately, it's the only test of its kind. It's imperfect, to be sure, but everyone knows that some lives have been saved because the test has been used. We just don't know who those people are. We also know some people have been hurt because they used the test and it was positive and they followed up and even in some cases died because of the treatment.

So we say that it's important that the clinician and the patient talk about this, that they be informed a test does exist, but there are definite risks and definite benefits. And at the end of the day, it should be between the doctor and his or her patient as to whether that test is used or not.

Senator ROBERTS. Thank you very much. I appreciate that. In your former role as Deputy Secretary at HHS, Dr. Troy, you oversaw the development and approval of regulations, all regulations, and significance guidance. That's a hell of a job. Can you speak to the use of interim final rules to implement specific policy priorities and comment on the use of an IFR to implement prevention priorities? And I'm very worried about IFRs becoming final without any comment period down the line, which I think is absolutely essential.

Mr. TROY. Thank you, Senator. IFRs, interim final rules, are an important tool in the tool chest of regulators. But they are a tool to be used sparingly. So to the extent that it is something——

Senator ROBERTS. Give me an example.

Mr. TROY. Well, if there's a national security concern, if you have to get a regulation out very quickly, that might be a good time to use an IFR. I think we may have used them in terms of bioterror or biopreparedness regulations. So it is not something that should be forbidden. It's in the APA, the Administrative Procedures Act.

But there should not be an over-reliance on IFRs, because, as you say, they do circumvent what you call in the Senate regular order, and so I am very worried about using them too much. And there has been a concern with the Affordable Care Act about the use of IFRs to get regulations out faster and to not get the notice and comments that's required.

Senator ROBERTS. So the IFR used to seek the end result of an agenda would not be helpful. In a specific instance where it obviously—you have to act in haste—then you would recommend that. I am just worried about IFRs being used too many times.

I yield back, Mr. Chairman.

The CHAIRMAN. Senator Whitehouse.

Senator WHITEHOUSE. Thank you, Chairman.

First, let me thank the Heart Association and the Cancer Society and the Diabetes Association for the work that you did as we were preparing for the Affordable Care Act with the joint statement that we worked on on healthcare delivery system reform. I think that when the three of you and the other illness advocacy groups get together, you can have very, very powerful effects. And I appreciate that you put the weight of your credibility and your energy as entities behind that effort. So let me just begin by thanking you.

You heard the questions that Senator Roberts and I had for Secretary Koh. I think you've got a very friendly audience here in terms of the wisdom and merit of prevention investment. But in order to get from being friendly into having real programs that really support this effort, we have to go through a fairly rigorous process of scoring and trying to work through that this actually will save money and trying to figure out when.

It strikes me that supporting that kind of initiative would be very valuable infrastructure for you in order to make these arguments more effective and allow us to deploy this more effectively as we go forward. I don't doubt for a moment that you're right and, frankly, we're all right about this subject.

But when you get to the details of which should be rolled out first, which will have the most immediate effect, which will have the most pronounced effect, how do you tell one from the other, where is the best way to put a fixed number of dollars, I think more rigor would advance all of our causes. And I'm interested in each of your thoughts on what you think the best mechanism would be for establishing that kind of cost-benefit rigor. And do you agree that if we had that improved, that would, in turn, improve our ability to get legislation and funding through this institution?

Ms. Brown first.

Ms. BROWN. Certainly, the point, Senator, is an excellent point. We at the American Heart Association believe that demonstrated outcomes is really critical for all of the work that we do. And I might mention, as one example, Dr. Koh was asked about the Million Hearts Initiative. We're very closely working with the Department of Health and Human Services and all of the agencies on Million Hearts.

And as a matter of fact, we'll be together, harmonizing the data so that the program of the American Heart Association, Cancer Society, and Diabetes Association, called the guideline advantage, can be used to collect data in communities to show the return on investment and value in investing these dollars of the Federal Government in saving a million heart attacks and strokes in the next 5 years. And so measurement and evaluation is a key part of that program.

One of the reasons we published a paper in circulation in July of this year looking at the cost-effectiveness of prevention is exactly to the kinds of questions that we've heard asked today. We get asked those questions all the time at the AHA as well, because we operate on donor dollars, and donors want to understand, just as the Federal Government does, that their dollars are being used to prevent heart disease and stroke.

And so in our paper we were able to demonstrate a number of ways that we can look at measuring the cost-effectiveness of prevention, and we'd be happy to share that.

Senator WHITEHOUSE. Dr. Seffrin.

Mr. SEFFRIN. I would certainly be appreciative of that point of view, and I think it's extremely important, and we should be as rigorous as we can be. I would only offer a cautionary note. If you look at the entire spectrum of interventions from primary public health to major league intensive care and treatment and medicines, you might be surprised how little rigor has been in some of those things that have been funded heavily over and over and over again. But I'm not arguing against rigor. I'm just saying that let's not be harder on prevention than we are on other areas with respect to health promotion.

The second point I would make——

Senator WHITEHOUSE. Particularly when you're only 1 to 4 percent of the healthcare dollar, with all the gain that can be made.

Mr. SEFFRIN. Exactly.

Senator WHITEHOUSE. I understand that.

Mr. SEFFRIN. Exactly.

Senator WHITEHOUSE. But this is less about the relative merits of one strategy versus another than it is about being able to move stuff through Congress——

Mr. SEFFRIN. Yes.

Senator WHITEHOUSE [continuing]. With the kind of cost justification that makes it easy to go rather than creating a quarrel over whether the cost justification is there or not.

Mr. SEFFRIN. There are some things, though, that I think about the breast and cervical cancer early detection program and the limited funding for that. We've been able to demonstrate and prove and publish literature of earlier detection and saving of lives. And the disparity issue—that would be an area that policymakers could invest a lot more money and get a tremendous return on that investment.

I think you can look at things that you know will be guaranteed, that will work. You can look at the Federal excise tax on tobacco and increase it by $2 a pack. I think that was recommended a number of years ago and never looked at seriously. You do that— you're going to get results, and it'll pay off.

Let me make one more point. I predict that within 24 to 36 months, the American Cancer Society will announce for the first time in the history of the republic a 20 percent reduction in age standardized cancer mortality rates in America. It's never happened before in the world, in any country.

Senator WHITEHOUSE. Repeat that again.

Mr. SEFFRIN. I predict that in 24 to 36 months, we'll be announcing a 20 percent reduction in age standardized cancer mortality rates in America. We already can show you that 900,000 people will have a birthday this year because they didn't die of cancer, that would have if the cancer death rates had stayed the same as they were in 1991. So that's why we say we're the official sponsor of birthdays.

Now, my point in all that, a very important point—we know that when we announce that, that is a $10 trillion economic yield to the American public. So it's not just about the cost of the program and what you get. It's also about the economic value of intervening and keeping people healthier longer.

So aging is a global phenomenon. And in 20 years we know precisely we're going to be 20 years older if we're still here. And we're either going to be 20 years older and productive or disabled, and if we're disabled, we've got a real economic problem on our hands.

Senator WHITEHOUSE. Mr. Chairman, my time has expired. I thank you.

The CHAIRMAN. Thank you, Senator Whitehouse.

Senator Blumenthal.

Senator BLUMENTHAL. Thank you, Mr. Chairman, and thank you for holding this hearing on a topic that I think we all agree is profoundly important, crucial to the future of healthcare and the health of our Nation.

I want to thank all of you for your very good work in this area.

Mr. Seffrin, I had a question about—and, by the way, thank you for your longstanding and continued work on tobacco cessation and prevention, which we began some years ago together when I was attorney general. I was interested in a statistic that you cited. I don't have it in front of me, but I believe it's that cessation quit lines could reach 16 percent of smokers annually.

Obviously, that's a lot better than 1 percent, but I was curious as to why it's not 50 percent or 60 percent, why it's only 16 percent. Maybe I misunderstand the statistic.

Mr. SEFFRIN. Well, it's resources, basically. We have a call center in Austin, TX, that we can answer your calls 24 hours a day, 7 days a week, and on all holidays. We have a quit line, but the key is that we can only service as many people as we have funds for. So there's no question in my mind that 16 percent could be doubled or tripled if the resources were there to pay for the service. As it turns out, quit lines are not particularly inexpensive.

Senator BLUMENTHAL. Well, I'm glad you clarified that, because I had understood that part of your testimony to indicate that that was the maximum, even with adequate funding, that could be covered. But I think that's important to recognize, that the only real limit is funding.

In fact, that was the experience in Connecticut. We had a quit line with pharmaceutical drugs. There was a reluctance to fund it, and it was exhausted within 30, 60 days. It was supposed to last for a year. So people want to quit, don't they?

Mr. SEFFRIN. Absolutely.

Senator BLUMENTHAL. That is really across the board the most enthusiastic anti-tobacco crusaders. Many of them are smokers who want to quit and have tried again and again and again and need some help to do so.

Mr. SEFFRIN. Absolutely correct.

Senator BLUMENTHAL. Dr. Troy, if I can ask you, I understand you have reservations about some of the anti-obesity efforts, the reliance on Shrek and on Curtis Granderson by the present administration. Do you have the same sorts of reservations about anti-tobacco efforts, that is, promotional and educational efforts aimed at young people to try to stop them from beginning to smoke?

Mr. TROY. Thank you for the question. I actually don't really have that many reservations about Shrek and Curtis Granderson. I happen to be a Yankee fan, and I'm all fine with that. I just don't think that they're that effective broadly. But, they don't spend that much government money, either, so they're not a big problem. I like the idea of using role models to help discourage kids from smoking, kids from overeating, and encouraging them to exercise.

Senator BLUMENTHAL. And, in fact, some of the most effective role models are used in so-called spit tobacco or chewing tobacco, as it's commonly known, where some of the sports stars who have used it and who have suffered or seen others suffer are, in effect, brought in front of classes or groups of young people and are tremendously effective in that regard, certainly much more effective than, I should say, even a U.S. Senator or an Attorney General lecturing them and preaching and so forth. But those role models are very important, aren't they?

Mr. TROY. I'm a big fan of the use of role models, and especially—I mean, it's tragic when you have these sports stars who have done that. Babe Ruth, for example, died of throat cancer from smoking too many cigars. It's tragic when you have that happen. But it is important if we can leverage these tragedies into getting good effects.

Senator BLUMENTHAL. Thank you very much.

Thank you to all of you for your great work in this area and thank you for being here today.

Thank you, Mr. Chairman.

The CHAIRMAN. Senator Franken.

Senator FRANKEN. This is for anyone on the panel. Is a hot workplace beneficial?

[Laughter.]

Mr. SEFFRIN. I don't think so.

Senator FRANKEN. OK.

Senator BLUMENTHAL. He didn't ask about hot air.

[Laughter.]

Senator FRANKEN. Mr. Griffin, I want to——

Senator ROBERTS. Would the Senator yield? Are you talking about this sauna bath we're in here or——

[Laughter.]

Senator FRANKEN. Yes, I was, I was.

Thank you, Mr. Griffin, for talking about the National Diabetes Prevention Program as a strong example of primary prevention. In your experience, what elements of this program make it so successful, and why should we be using limited Federal dollars to fund it?

Mr. GRIFFIN. Well, it answers Senator Whitehouse's question and Senator Roberts, because it's built on actual dollars. It's built on actual outcomes. These programs started with the NIH, with actual clinical trials, translated into community-based programs that led to the legislation that you and Senator Lugar proposed. The cost, as we shared, is $300 per person to keep them out of the circle of those with diabetes or full-blown diabetes, part of the 26 million.

Senator FRANKEN. I think the average to treat someone with diabetes a year is about $6,000. Is that about right?

Mr. GRIFFIN. That's right. And within that $6,000 are countless, needless surgeries, hours of kidney dialysis, and amputations within that. We know from the Urban Institute by taking that $300—when we talk about cost-effectiveness, that $300 keeps a third of those folks out of the diabetes community—that we save $190 billion over 10 years. Those are inevitable surgeries. Those one out of three Medicare dollars are going for surgeries, eye surgeries, amputations that are very expensive, and they are human tragedies as well as financial ones.

This is one area where Congress has required scientific rigor in the clinical trials at NIH and demonstrated it in a community setting on a trial basis. Our only problem is that if we could replicate it—not just in YMCAs where they are now, the Y's. If we get them around the country, that's where that $190 billion savings can be actually attained and procedures averted that are otherwise going to overwhelm the healthcare system. We cannot afford in the next 25 years to take care of complications in that expensive manner.

Senator FRANKEN. I want to thank you for sharing the story of my constituent, Margaret Hutchinson. It's really inspiring to see these folks go through this program and come out with weight loss and with just a better life. I was talking with General Shinseki, the Veterans Affairs Secretary. He visited Minnesota in August. And I learned that diabetes affects more than 1 million veterans.

You, obviously, share the belief that we should make this more accessible to veterans and the elderly, and the elderly have a higher success rate, actually, with the National Diabetes Prevention Plan. Right?

Mr. GRIFFIN. Seventy-one percent, even more than the 60 percent of others. That's right, Senator.

Senator FRANKEN. I have one question for Dr. Troy, which is, Do you know what the experience has been in Massachusetts?

Mr. TROY. I believe you had more companies covering. But the structure is slightly different. And there was a study in the *Wall Street Journal* that showed that AT&T, for example, spends about $2.2 billion annually on covering its workers——

Senator FRANKEN. Do you know the number of companies covering?

Mr. TROY. I don't know the exact number, although I can send it to you after, if you want, although I still don't know.

Senator FRANKEN. Well, I do. It's the highest in the country. Seventy-six percent of Massachusetts companies now cover their employees. In fact, I believe it's the only State since 2006, when their mandate went into effect, where companies have increased—in every other State in the country, it has gone down.

So I don't understand, did the *Wall Street Journal* have a study or an editorial?

Mr. TROY. It was a statistic cited in the *Wall Street Journal*.

Senator FRANKEN. Cited where in the *Wall Street Journal*?

Mr. TROY. It was on the editorial page—an op-ed.

Senator FRANKEN. On the editorial page.

Mr. TROY. It was an op-ed.

Senator FRANKEN. OK. It was an op-ed——

Mr. TROY. Yes.

Senator FRANKEN [continuing]. in the *Wall Street Journal*.

Mr. TROY. Yes.

Senator FRANKEN. That's interesting.

Mr. TROY. But the statistic remains accurate.

Senator FRANKEN. Thank you, Mr. Chairman.

[Laughter.]

Mr. TROY. May I respond?

Senator FRANKEN. Yes, you can respond to that. Sure.

Mr. TROY. I just wanted to say what the statistic was, which was that about $2.2 billion is spent by AT&T on providing healthcare for its workers, and they calculated that it would cost $600 million for them to dump their employees and pay the penalty. Now, I personally don't think that AT&T might make that calculation, because they're heavily in the public eye. But other companies might look at—less prominent companies might look at that spread, that $1.6 billion spread——

Senator FRANKEN. Oh, I'd love to respond to your comment on that statistic, because the point is—the same is true in Massachusetts. These companies easily could have dropped their employees and saved money. What they discovered was that to keep valuable employees, they wanted to cover them, and it became expected for companies to cover them.

Mr. Chairman.

The CHAIRMAN. Listen, I have a couple more questions I would like to followup on.

Mr. Griffin, you've talked about the Diabetes Prevention Program. Why do you think this program is more cost-effective at the community level than similar programs that use a one-on-one physician-patient approach? Why is that different?

Mr. GRIFFIN. The primary care system is ill-equipped to help a person who is in the zone of danger for diabetes. Patients that—the physicians, even diabetes educators—we do not have enough of them. They are not in the mainstream of people's lives in our communities in our country.

The Y, for example, in most communities is a well-respected organization with good standards. They're science-based. People are comfortable. It works. We know that physicians—if they could take one or two out of three of their patients who are pre-diabetic and take them outside the zone of danger, they would, but they can't. We know the Y has done a better job in a patient's own community at keeping them outside the circle of diabetes. That's where we want to keep them.

And we know—everybody at this table agrees we want people more fit—better nutrition, more exercise and physical activity. These programs work to do just that. They begin more physical activity. They lose weight. Their blood glucose goes down. The corresponding benefits are hypertension is lowered in those populations. We've proven both in the science, in the clinical part of it, that it works.

It's been translated into community-based programs, which have been funded on a trial basis by this Congress in a bipartisan way. It works. It works in a myriad of ways, and it needs to be nationwide.

The CHAIRMAN. Let me focus on one other thing. Dr. Troy had an interesting thing in his testimony. He said that the Army found that 27 percent—you mentioned that—of its recruits were unfit, too overweight to serve in the military.

"Retired Rear Admiral James Barnett put the issue starkly, warning that our national security in 2030 is absolutely dependent on reversing the alarming rates of child obesity."

OK. I want to know how—how do we do this? Do you have any thoughts, any ideas you can share with us on how we get—especially in the minority communities that we know—and Hispanics. Well, how do we help there? How do we do that? Or do we just throw up our hands and say it can't be done? What do we do?

Mr. GRIFFIN. Well, the association—what we've done is gone around to school campuses, getting those sugar sweetened beverages out of those campuses and encouraging—or not just encouraging—actually, in some States, mandating that schools have healthy choices available for those kids. We also know from our experience with the Diabetes Prevention Program that those parents who are educated as to nutrition and fitness—they are going to take that to the next generation of children.

My sister is a pediatrician. She sees obese kids. When the parents get the training on nutrition, when they get community-based training, they can help with the next generation as well. But, clearly, that is a problem.

And we are fortunate—as one of my colleagues just said this—that the First Lady, in terms of making that a priority in large companies, Wal-Mart, other places where she's worked, as well as on school campuses—that is a way to intervene, because children don't have any choice—the kinds of beverages that adults put in front of them when they're small.

The CHAIRMAN. Well, we know one of the successes—the success of public health in America has been through outreach and community involvement. It seems like in the past we've done a good job with that in terms of certain specific interventions, immunizations, things like that.

But we haven't done a very good job of it in terms of broad-based interventions in terms of diet, exercise—well, we've done some on smoking. Some good interventions have been done on smoking. But just diet and exercise—for example, what kids should be eating, how parents can reinforce one another to have healthy meals in schools. I've been fighting for years. In the 1996 Farm bill, I first introduced an amendment to get vending machines taken out of schools, and you see I was a spectacular failure at that one.

But we have made progress. We're now getting the sugary drinks out and the candy and stuff like that out. We're finally getting there on that. But we need better thoughts and better ideas on how we involve the community. And I'm thinking now of the community of Hispanics and Latinos in this country, the African-American community—for interventions and self-reinforcement in that community. And I'm just open for thoughts and suggestions on how we do that.

Ms. Brown.

Ms. BROWN. To follow Dr. Koh's earlier testimony, two of the important components of the Prevention Fund are the Community

Transformation Grants and the communities putting prevention to work. And one of the really spectacular components of those programs are that communities themselves are looking at the issues that they're facing, whether it's a high ethnic minority population or a more affluent population, whatever their situation might be.

And they are identifying needs, coming together with multiple stakeholders in a community, creating innovative ideas and submitting them for funding that go through this very rigorous peer review process that Dr. Koh identified. Therein we will find many solutions that we can replicate in other communities throughout the country. That's one thing that I would mention.

The other thing I would say—several years ago, the American Heart Association co-created the Alliance for a Healthier Generation, which is focused on the issue of childhood obesity, with the Clinton Foundation. And we have worked in low-income schools throughout this country and demonstrated with data collection a reduced rate of obesity in kids, more physical activity, and it certainly helps to incorporate families, teachers in creating a full environment that promotes optimal health at a young age.

The CHAIRMAN. I'm just seeing if there's any other thoughts on these community-based involvements.

Dr. Troy.

Mr. TROY. Yes. This is a real challenge, what you raised about childhood obesity and how to address the questions when children are obese, because you cannot apply economic incentives there, and it's very hard to get in the home and tell parents what to do. One study I found in my research on this—and it was not in the *Wall Street Journal*, although I think it's a perfectly legitimate place for studies. But this was a study at the University of Illinois that found that a college graduate is 12 to 28 percent less likely to be obese than a similar person with just a high school degree.

So that goes across demographic groups. It's not just within one demographic group or one class. So I'm not saying that everybody needs to go to college or everybody can go to college. But there is something about that higher education that seems to promote lower obesity rates, and I was wondering if we could study that and see what about the socialization you get in higher education that we could apply to the parents who would then hopefully apply it to their children.

The CHAIRMAN. I would wonder how much correlation there is in that data with income, where they fall on the poverty-wealth scale.

Mr. TROY. Right. And the key point is that—than a similar person with a high school degree. So it applies across groups. Now, obviously, people with a higher education do skew wealthier. But what this study was comparing is people across groups—people of lower income who get a college degree to people of lower income who get just a high school degree.

The CHAIRMAN. It's just that people of low income tend to have bad diets. Now, why do people of low income have bad diets? As Michael Pollan pointed out in his book, he began to think about that. And he went in the grocery store and found out that poor people buy with food stamps, the SNAP program and others. They tend to buy foods that are high in sugars, fats, and starches.

Why do they do that? Because they're the cheapest. Why are they the cheapest? Because we subsidize those the most in agriculture, not fruits and vegetables. We don't subsidize those, but we subsidize starches, fats, and sugars, so they're cheap, and so people go and buy them. If you're pinching pennies, you don't go to the fresh fruit and the fresh produce counter. You buy packaged products. They're very cheap—high in sodium, too, by the way, very high in sodium.

So we're trying some things. We tried some things in the last Farm bill to try to get more fresh fruits, fresh vegetables to those food deserts, as they say in the inner cities and things. But, again, it seems to me that this is a public health problem. No question it's a public health problem. And why shouldn't we be approaching it that way?

Dr. Seffrin.

Mr. SEFFRIN. We should, and you're absolutely correct. The most sobering thing for me in my life—because we know the association between obesity and cancer, not one cancer but many cancers. But the other point that's been made is how much it involves all three of these major diseases, heart disease, diabetes, and cancer.

The most sobering thing and why I say, prevention is the best policy, is that we have very little evidence that we can do much about morbid obesity once it occurs. When the best thing you can do is cover gastric surgery at $25,000 a pop—and one State, California, has over a million people who would qualify under Medicare to have that—that's a pretty sobering reality about what we know to do.

On the other hand, over 90 percent of our neonates are born healthy.

The CHAIRMAN. Say that again.

Mr. SEFFRIN. Over 90 percent—in America, in this great country, over 90 percent of newborn babies are born healthy. And neonatal birth weights have not changed in over 300 years. So we know this is an environmental problem and a policy issue. We have to look at some of the good old days. You know, we used to have exercise in school classes and physical education and health education.

What I'm saying is I think it's complex and we don't have exact answers, because we haven't been very effective at controlling it. But it is a threat to this Nation's future economic and public health stability. And policies need to be developed to change the environment so kids are encouraged to stay healthy.

Over 90 percent of those neonates are born healthy, and most—not all—most are genetically programmed to stay healthy for a normal human life span. And we need to create an environment that encourages the kind of behaviors and practices that would make that come true.

Mr. GRIFFIN. There's been a thoughtful discussion, Senator, among these three organizations and others about increasing the percentages of children's diet that is—the sugar they get is close to a third, just from sugar sweetened beverages. That's a third of all of their sugar just from that one source. It's a problem.

So there is a thoughtful discussion about taxing the heck out of them. I mean, we have a task force at the ADA right now studying sugar sweetened beverages and how do we lower its consumption by young people, because that's why they are obese.

The CHAIRMAN. That's right.

Mr. GRIFFIN. On the other hand, we know through the programs that Congress has supported, through the Special Diabetes Prevention Program, that when people can get counseling on nutrition and fitness in their own communities where they live and play, it works. And it covers more than one generation, because once they've been sensitized to that fact that we just talked about, that a fourth of calories that are from those beverages alone contributing to obesity and cancer and heart disease, we can make a difference. And so we have to eliminate barriers to people having a good understanding of both fitness and nutrition in their home neighborhood.

The CHAIRMAN. I appreciate you saying that. That was the thought processes and the discussion that went on in setting up these Community Transformation Grants—not that the government has all the answers. We don't—but providing some framework for communities to get together and discover their own ways of doing things and coming—a lot of times, people say, "Well, what you're talking about is common sense."

Well, yes, it's common sense, but until you get people together in groups and have these supporting elements in communities, where they recognize it's a community problem, common sense kind of goes out the window, because people are sort of by themselves out there, and they don't know what they need to do. But with the Community Transformation Grants, you encourage them to come up with their own solutions.

Mr. GRIFFIN. That's right, but outcome-based. Like the programs at the Y.

The CHAIRMAN. I want it outcome-based, and I want to know which ones work best.

Mr. GRIFFIN. Right. Exactly.

The CHAIRMAN. I diverge a little bit from some of my colleagues who said we don't want to put money in anything that's not proven. Well, I'd like to test some theories out. I'd like to see maybe if somebody's got some ideas, if some communities have an idea out there on doing something that hasn't been done before. OK. Let's see if it works.

Maybe somebody's got a better idea out there. And why should we be constrained by just the narrow things of what we know that works? Maybe there are other things out there that will work. So that's why I've been very promotive of getting communities to come up with new ideas and new approaches on this.

Well, it's been a great discussion. I'm sorry, Senator Roberts. I yield to you.

Senator ROBERTS. Your recommendation is we increase taxes on sugar products in regards to the soft drink industry and also on tobacco? Is that correct?

Mr. GRIFFIN. Dr. Seffrin has already talked about the increase in cigarette prices, in terms of the decrease in the use. Yes, there are plenty of studies that show that there will be decreased consumption of sugar sweetened beverages if the price goes up.

We have a task force currently that will—by gosh, at the end of my term as chair of the board, we will have a policy by the end of the year come hell or high water. But we are currently studying the precise ways in which we can decrease consumption.

Two of those methods being considered is allowing the States to tax at a higher rate sugar sweetened beverages, and also a subject that's on the table—very controversial—people are thinking about it—is whether the SNAP program ought to be adjusted so as participants in that program would not be able to utilize the food stamp dollars to purchase those sorts of beverages.

Senator ROBERTS. Now, that's an argument that's been going on for some years.

Mr. GRIFFIN. It has. But as long as our children are obese, we are going to continue to have that discussion——

Senator ROBERTS. Or more obese.

Mr. GRIFFIN. Or more obese—until that trajectory goes the other way. And there is a sense of—how should I put this—restlessness in the American people, at least in the 26 million people in my community, and I'm sure it's the same in Cancer and Heart. We want to make a dent in that. We want that dent to happen sooner rather than later.

Senator ROBERTS. I don't know. Maybe it's because I come from a—very fortunate. I didn't think so at the time—being raised in a small community. And so there was mandatory gym in high school, I think, when we were there, Mr. Chairman. Maybe not. Maybe we have an age difference I'm not aware of.

But at any rate, there was mandatory gym. YMCA—we took a bus down to Topeka and learned how to swim. It was mandatory. I'm not quite sure why it was mandatory or who said it was mandatory, but that's what we did. I learned how to swim. It's a very easy process. They throw you in the deep end and say, "Swim." That was a little harsh, but you do dog paddle back to the side. And, of course, you probably fear water after that, but that's beside the point.

There are a lot of activities that were going on in the small town where I grew up during that era.

Mr. GRIFFIN. That was a whole different era.

Senator ROBERTS. I understand that. And I have no trouble, some of the time, thinking is this really the Federal Government's responsibility to suggest—and it is suggest, not coerce or mandate—local communities to do X, Y, or Z. I don't think that's the answer. I think it is to try to network and say, "All right. This works. This doesn't. Why don't you give this a try, et cetera, et cetera"—leave it up to the States and the local communities.

But I was just interested in your recommendations on tax policy. Does that come in on the 9–9–9 program, or is that——

[Laughter.]

All right. I'm sorry. I'm not behaving.

Mr. GRIFFIN. We're not at Dartmouth anymore, Senator Roberts.

Senator ROBERTS. Thank you.

Mr. GRIFFIN. I'm just teasing.

Senator ROBERTS. Thank you all for your commentary and the work you're doing. Thank you so much.

The CHAIRMAN. Thank you all. It was a great panel and great testimony. I think we had a great exchange here. I request that the record be kept open for 10 days until all Senators submit statements and questions for the record.

Again, thank you all very much for this, and thank you for all the work you do on the outside too.

[Additional material follows.]

ADDITIONAL MATERIAL

PREPARED STATEMENT OF SENATOR ENZI

I would like to thank the Chairman for his continued focus on chronic disease prevention. Our Nation has a problem with obesity and chronic diseases, like cardiovascular disease, diabetes, and cancer. The numbers speak for themselves—according to CDC, 7 out of 10 deaths among Americans each year are from chronic diseases.

Equally alarming is the rate of childhood obesity, which has tripled in the last 30 years. The military is reporting problems with recruiting because people don't qualify on the fitness exams. Given these daunting statistics and accounts, it is imperative that we come together to address these problems. I fear the costs, both economic and otherwise, if we do not.

What we need are solid, evidence-based proposals that encourage people to take their health into their own hands. We all know that individual behaviors and lifestyle choices can have an impact on either preventing these diseases from occurring or reducing their severity. Wellness programs are an excellent way to incentivize healthy behaviors. Employers have been looking to such programs to improve the health of their employees and keep costs down. Safeway's CEO, Steven Burd, has testified before this committee about the successes his company has with its wellness program. I am encouraged by these kinds of innovative ideas, and I look forward to hearing about more ways that we can address this problem.

What we don't need is to continue spending billions of dollars to fund initiatives that restrict our ability to make our own decisions. I'm concerned that in a time of record deficits, we see the Secretary accepting recommendations for coverage without cost sharing—without any analysis on what the effect will be on the budget. In the past, CBO has said that a number of preventive services add cost rather than savings. I am not saying the recommendations are with or without merit—simply that to not even consider the impact on the budget is irresponsible.

Actions like this increase my concerns about the use of the billions of dollars in the prevention fund. With little to no accountability, this massive fund provides the Secretary with unprecedented ability to dispense funds at her discretion. The lack of accountability is alarming. In this budget environment, we have to make careful decisions about how and where we prioritize funding. The Fund allows the Secretary to fund programs and initiatives over and above the amount Congress deliberated over and allocated money for.

I am looking forward to hearing from Dr. Koh about how the Fund is being used, and how it has improved health and reduced public and private health care costs. We've got to make sure that spending on prevention programs is evidence-based and targeted with clear metrics on success.

No one is denying that chronic disease is an issue on a massive scale, and I anticipate that our witnesses will provide sobering testimony on the state of chronic disease in the United States. Scientists, medical professionals, public health workers, policymakers, and even economists have been working to prevent and treat chronic diseases. I commend them for their tireless devotion to this problem facing our country.

I have been working on ways to fix our broken healthcare system for well over a decade now. One of the chronic problems I've encountered time and time again is proposals that do nothing to lower health care costs and instead, in fact, dramatically increase health care spending. We can't keep doing things the Washington way, passing the buck, literally, to the next generation. The American people are calling for us to look at spending, look at the debt, and do something about it. We can, and should do better. I look forward to hearing from our witnesses, and thank them for taking the time to be here today.

[Whereupon, at 4:41 p.m., the hearing was adjourned.]

○